Thi D1582791 fore

THE DREAMING SWIMMER

non-fiction 1987–1992

CLIVE JAMES

JONATHAN CAPE
LONDON

First published 1992
© Clive James 1992
Jonathan Cape, 20 Vauxhall Bridge Road, London SWIV 2SA

Clive James has asserted his right under
the Copyright, Designs and Patents Act, 1988
to be identified as the author of this work

A CIP catalogue record for this book
is available from the British Library

ISBN 0–224–03602–5

Photoset by Falcon Graphic Art Ltd
Wallington, Surrey
Printed in Great Britain by
Mackays of Chatham PLC, Chatham, Kent

to the memory of
Janet Evans

nobis cum semel occidit brevis lux
nox est perpetua una dormienda

The striking aphorism requires a stricken aphorist.
– Alfred Polgar

Acknowledgment is due to the editors of the *New Yorker*, the *London Review of Books*, *The Times Literary Supplement*, the *Observer*, the *Spectator* and the *Radio Times*, in which some of these pieces first appeared; to the controlling bodies of ITV, the BBC and the Royal Television Society for asking my opinion; and to Joanna Kilmartin, Sarah Raphael, Pete Atkin and Billy Connolly for choosing me as a spokesman.

Contents

Introduction

Even in America, only the specialist student of the Algonquin circle would nowadays recognise the name of Alexander Woollcott, and only the specialist in Alexander Woollcott would remember a line he wrote. Fluent without talent – perhaps the most enviable talent of all – he had, however, celebrity. Wolcott Gibbs hadn't, though he wrote with the easy-seeming colloquial snap for which Alexander Woollcott could offer only jocose verbosity as a substitute. Today, with his achievements, if they are mentioned at all, invariably attributed to his giftless near-namesake, Wolcott Gibbs is a separate identity only for the reader who believes that a serious note can be struck in casual journalism, and struck most truly when the touch is light.

But for any reader who does believe that, Wolcott Gibbs is important. More than thirty years ago, when I was majoring in extracurricular activities at the University of Sydney, I committed his collection of pieces called *Season in the Sun* to memory. Today I own both the American and British editions and would buy every second-hand copy of the book I came across if that did not mean depriving some young browser of the same discovery. Gibbs's profile of Henry Luce, written in a parody of early *Time* style and featuring the much-misquoted tag-line 'Backwards run sentences until reels the mind', pioneered a form of criticism in which he had many imitators but no peers. His book reviews amusingly exposed the gap between ambition and attainment. He was a truly witty theatre critic where Dorothy Parker was merely witty at theatre's expense. In my opinion, freely given to my fellow aspirants on the staff of the Sydney University newspaper *honi soit*, Gibbs ranked with A. J. Liebling and S. J. Perelman among the *New Yorker* writers who had transcended the house style and made the voice of America their own. They all collected pieces rather than wrote books.

The same was also true of most of my old world models. George Bernard Shaw's six Standard Edition volumes of music and theatre criticism constituted, for at least one admirer who would read aloud from them at parties unless forced not to, the most powerful single recommendation for a practical critical engagement, as opposed to an academic detachment. Later on I mustered some appreciation for academic detachment as well, but when young and more impatient I liked the immediacy, the quotability, and, of course, the brevity, of the periodical article written to a tight deadline. Even Shaw's marathon critical effort was really just a collection of weekly columns. His creative personality gave it coherence. It still does, when so many of his plays lie dead. I can't imagine ever wanting to read the preface to *Man and Superman* again, but I still return to *Our Theatres in the Nineties*, and find it just as difficult now as long ago to read five pages without reading fifty.

In the ensuing decades I have built, without really trying to, a whole library of critical works – weighted inevitably, the times being what they are, towards the scholarly and the academic. But at the heart of it, and among my favourite books of any kind, are those books that the conventional wisdom would have us believe are not *really* books at all. Some of them – for example Edmund Wilson's two key collections *The Shores of Light* and *Classics and Commercials* – are simply the richest concentrations of critical thought in modern times. Of those, most would never have been published if the publishers had shared the conviction, nowadays most often propagated by book reviewers themselves, that collections of reviews are to be deplored. No opportunity should be lost to condemn that view as illiterate. As publishers become more reluctant to amortise a low-selling book against a high-selling one, even if they are both by the same author, it needs to be emphasised that some of the best non-fiction books are composed from casual journalism. It should also be said that the prospect of being able to republish their work in a collection was one of the things that used to make casual journalists write with care. The reviewer who dismisses his colleague's collection of articles as a pretentious claim on posterity would sound more persuasive if his review were energised by the same ambition. But increasingly it isn't written to last the time it takes to read it. London literary journalism has not benefited from so easily accepting its latter-day status as irredeemable ephemera. The result, ever more in the ascendant, has been a kind of ignorant knowingness, a whole new brand of aggressive modesty. I preferred the old conceit, which the first section of this book is unapologetically intended to perpetuate.

The second section is the product of strange circumstances. Since Mrs Thatcher launched her mischievous assault on Britain's broadcasting system, nobody living in the target area has been able to escape involvement with the underlying politics of an institution vital not just to this nation but – surely the claim is not too large – to the world entire. Ordinarily it would have been sufficient commitment just to make the best possible programmes, which need a long week's work for a good half hour, and absorb more energy the easier they look. But morale in the broadcasting system collapsed so rapidly under the government's attack that it became a dereliction not to engage in polemics. Against my inclination, I found myself making speeches. It simply had to be done, ready or not, win or – more likely – lose. Where politics is concerned, in the margin of history (Sir Lewis Namier's excellent title for one of his several lastingly instructive collections of essays) is where I prefer to be. This one time I was mixed up in the action. For the theoretical treatise about television I might have written in an ideal academic world, these pieces are the contingent, shop-soiled substitute. Composed on trains and in the backs of cars, typed late at night when I should have been asleep, they are not without deficiencies, and may well be without virtues. But they took all I had at the time, so I am betting that some of the urgency still comes through, if only as a sense of strain.

The third section consists of non-fiction in verse form: pieces which would have had to wait a long time for my next collection of poems, but which I was keen to see safely under cover. Mixing prose and verse in a single collection is not without precedent. In the pre-Nazi German-speaking world, a rich culture which included the dismembered but still productive Austro-Hungarian empire, there was an agreeably easygoing tradition by which the *Kleinkunst* practitioners would from time to time publish mixed collections of their recent periodical writings: *feuilletons*, reviews, sketches, aphorisms and poems all cohabiting on the untroubled assumption that the reader cared less about categories than about what the individual writer had been up to lately. Republished post-war as part of a determined but forlorn effort to put a shattered civilisation back together, the same material was tidily sorted out into its appropriate genres, leaving once unclassifiable writers looking dauntingly monumental – a polite way of saying dead, which most of them were, and prematurely at that. Glad to possess such thoroughgoing multi-volume standard editions, I still prefer those first, airy, disordered little volumes, which I search out all over the world in the cities to which the refugees fled and where their children, having grown up understandably alienated from the old language, sold the books. I find them with cracked hinges, stacked spine-up on the floors of airless rooms in New York, Los Angeles, Tel Aviv and Jerusalem: Kurt Tucholsky, Alfred Polgar, Egon Friedell, Alfred Kerr, Egon Kisch, Anton Kuh – light stylists of the heavy heart, their sentences, which once sped too fast to be weighed, caught between covers like cosmic rays in a bubble chamber.

Until recently the same sort of one-man cabaret book could be done in Britain too. Paul Dehn's *For Love and Money* has been with me for thirty years: reviews, essays, lampoons and poems all packed tight into one little volume, and yet somehow constantly shifting to illuminate one another from an unexpected angle. Dehn, the inheritor of James Agate's library, eventually vanished into affluence as a screen writer (*The Spy Who Came In From the Cold*, *The Deadly Affair*), but his early pieces, whether in paragraphs or stanzas, were individual in every phrase. Urbane, well-informed, elegant without being precious, it was the kind of writing which the influence of Dr Leavis scared out of the courtyard, to our lasting harm. Without Dehn's film reviews, my own television column would not have taken quite the tone it did. He was only one of a dozen influences – if there isn't more than one influence you can't be influenced – but he was crucial, because he showed how learning could be brought to bear in defence of simplicity, and that the only attack worth launching is in defence of a value. My biggest and perhaps most presumptuous ambition as a writer of fugitive pieces is that they might have the same enabling effect on the expectations of some up-and-coming young critic as Paul Dehn's once did on mine.

The last section might look like blatant self-publicity but I can only plead that the self being publicised is a performer, who must bark for his act if the press won't do it for him. When I began presenting full-scale television programmes I soon found that there was no point giving a round of interviews and profiles in the hope of a plug. That approach had long since ceased to be rewarding when it was time to publish a new book. To expect helpful coverage for a new TV show was to go too often to a well that was already poisoned. I don't, except in weak moments, blame journalists, to whose ranks I belong. But if I am not interested in talking about my private life, and the profile-writers are not interested in talking about my work, then there is nowhere for them to escape except into speculation. I bore them towards fantasy, which accumulates in the clippings file, hardening into myth under the pressure of its own weight. Thus, on the mercifully sparse occasions when it is my turn to be turned over, I get a chance to read about some calculating poseur who will do anything to display his erudition, while simultaneously plunging ruthlessly down-market in search of viewers. How anyone could successfully do both those things at once is hard to fathom, but perhaps they mean that I am doing it unsuccessfully.

Meanwhile I have to publicise my upcoming programmes somehow: the BBC isn't giving me all that air-time just to be coy. So when the editor of the *Radio Times* asks for six hundred words he gets the piece as quickly as I can do it. But that still means as quickly as I can do it well. As with any other writing task, you can write it to throw away or you can try to make it stick. For millions of readers who are mostly too busy during the day to build up a stock of obscure cultural references, I must strive to express myself in as unadorned a way as possible while being entertaining enough to ram home the message that their lives will be blighted if they don't see the show. Vulgarity is always a hazard. But if the flyer is sometimes garish, for the circus I make no excuse. Television for the mass audience is part of my vocation. I didn't choose to do it out of calculation; I am compelled to do it out of impulse. I sometimes hear about a version of myself who is pitifully unaware of the discrepancy between literary criticism for the discerning minority and mass-channel spectacle for the viewing public. I don't believe in that gap but wouldn't care if it were an abyss. What could I do if I fell in except try to make the fall look live a dive?

London, 1992

Part One:

ASSESSMENTS AND CELEBRATIONS

Not Drowning But Waving

(*Stevie: A Biography of Stevie Smith* by Jack Barbera and
William McBrien, Papermac, 1986)

S OME WOULD say that Stevie Smith was as daft as a
brush. Others would say that she was pretty much
of a bitch. Calling her mad was always the best way
to get out of admitting that she could be cruel, just as
calling her naïve was always the best way to get out of
admitting that her poetry made almost everybody else's
sound overwrought. It was an effect she intended, and
was not above occasionally crowing about.

> Many of the English,
> The intelligent English,
> Of the Arts, the Professions
>   and the Upper Middle Classes,
> Are under-cover men,
> But what is under the cover
> (That was original)
> Died . . .

Few people except the Queen, who gave her a medal and
asked her to tea, were brave enough to let on in public that
Stevie Smith's poetry was the kind they liked best because
it didn't sound like poetry at all. In private, however, she
always had a following, which in her later years grew to
embrace a large minority of Britain's intelligent readers,
so that she became something of a living treasure. Sir
John Betjeman was more widely loved – he was more
lovable – but the bookish were proud of Stevie as the
British sometimes are of an old concrete pillbox that is
allowed to go on disfiguring an otherwise perfect cow

3

pasture because it reminds them of a time when they felt united.

> Perhaps England our darling will
>   recover her lost thought
> We must think sensibly about our
>   victory and not be distraught,
> Perhaps America will have an idea,
>   and perhaps not.

She fitted in by not fitting in at all. Least of all did she fit into modern literary history, and that is probably why there has always been a certain amount of interest in her across the Atlantic from where she lived and wrote. Some of the brighter young American academics, hankering for a less deterministic version of their subject, would like to see it refocused on the individual talent. A more individual talent than Stevie Smith's you don't get.

This excellent biography originated in the United States. Its authors cherish Stevie in the same intense way as those American liberal-arts professors on sabbatical leave who, having booked into a different West End theatrical production every night, end up, sometimes at the expense of their judgment, more in love with London than anyone who lives there could ever be. But the tireless Messrs Barbera and McBrien – they even sound like a pair of sleuths – have cracked the case. They have fallen all the way for Stevie's marvellous spontaneity without being seduced by that little-girl act of hers or overawed by the ostentatiously suicidal *Weltschmerz* that for most of her long adult life made it seem unlikely she would get through another day without trying to end it all under a bus. To what degree her naïveté was false and her vulnerability tougher *au fond* than an old boot will remain conjectural, although nobody from now on will want to conjecture without adducing at least some of the evidence that Barbera and McBrien so meticulously provide. But there cannot now be, if there ever was, any doubt about her poetry. It was never naïve and seldom out of control. Stevie Smith was an artist of the utmost

4

sophistication, pursuing the classic course of returning to simplicity through refinement, calculating her linguistic effects with such precision that they sound as innocently commanding as a baby's cry in the night.

> Nobody heard him, the dead man,
> But still he lay moaning:
> I was much further out than you thought
> And not waving but drowning.

Stevie spent most of her almost seventy years looking after her aunt in Palmers Green, which in the course of time graduated from being near London to being well inside it but without getting any closer to the centre of the literary action. She would journey in by public transport to her stuffy job as secretary to a publisher, and, at the end of a tiresome day, journey back out again. Weekends in the country – she had Rilke's knack for securing invitations, although nothing like his punctilio as a guest – provided what little adventure she ever knew. Her pre-war *Novel on Yellow Paper* (an unforgettable work that has nevertheless needed to be rediscovered several times since the day it was first greeted, correctly, as a masterpiece) contains most of whatever had happened to her up until then, and altogether too much of what had happened to her friends, some of whom never forgave her for putting embarrassing facts unaltered into her fiction. She had been to Germany and found out something about it, although not enough to help her realise that the old-style anti-Semitism of Hilaire Belloc had irrevocably lost whatever charm it had ever had. For a while she was fashionable, but she did not live fashionably. On those smart country weekends her only function was that of spare wheel. Her sexuality was either infantile or uncommonly well hidden for someone who made a practice of saying unfortunate things. What she really knew about was books.

She read prodigiously, absorbing the whole of English poetry right down to the level of its technique. At school,

she had been obliged to get poems by heart. Sayability
was her criterion, even during the ten years it took her
to find her own voice. After she found it, she never wrote
a line that could not be read aloud by a bright child. No
child, though, has ever had her range of allusion. In *Novel
on Yellow Paper* the narrator – called Pompey but otherwise
indistinguishable from the actual Stevie – wonders whether
she has read too much. Stevie probably did read too much
for her own happiness, but for her poetry the result was a
well of association sunk through centuries. She also read
a great deal outside English, particularly in French, and
especially Racine, whose decorous example helped inspire
the finely calibrated play of tone which permitted her to
run wild in an ordered manner. A line of hers may look
as shapeless as a holdall but it can take a long time to
unpack.

> Come death, you know you must come
>   when you're called
> Although you're a god.

It is meant to be Dido speaking, but you can't, and
aren't meant to, read the words 'Come death' without
thinking of the song 'Come away, come away, death' in
Twelfth Night. On the page opposite 'Dido's Farewell to
Aeneas' in the *Collected Poems* (Oxford, 1976), the first line
of 'Childe Rolandine' shows how the frame she constructed
for her seemingly primitive pictures was, in the strict sense,
a frame of reference:

> Dark was the day for Childe Rolandine the artist
> When she went to work as a secretary-typist . . .

It was a dark tower to which Shakespeare's – and,
later, Browning's – Childe Roland heroically came. Stevie,
unheroically rotting behind a secretarial desk, has found
a way to raise her lament beyond the personal. In this
borrowed poetic context, a prosaic complaint brings the
reader bang up to date:

6

> It is the privilege of the rich
> To waste the time of the poor . . .

Throughout her work, free-verse poems alternate with more formal compositions, but the free verse always gestures toward form and the forms always wander off. She strove industriously to make it look as if she didn't quite know what she was doing. She knew exactly. Her poetry has the vivid appeal of the Douanier Rousseau's pictures or Mussorgsky's music, but where they lacked schooling she only pretended to lack it. Closer analogies would be with Picasso painting clowns or Stravinsky writing ballets. She knew everything about how poetry had sounded in the past, and could assemble echoes with the assurance of any other modern artist. Clearly, her historicism was, in her own mind, the enabling justification for plain utterance. How the two things were technically connected is more problematic. When she uses the cadences of the Bible to promote her atheism, the trick is obvious, but often the most an admiring reader can do is ruefully admit that she somehow reminds him of every poet since Chaucer while speaking so naturally that she might be just coming round from a general anaesthetic.

'Not waving but drowning' was, and remains, her most famous line. No doubt the Queen asked her about it while pouring the tea. After a long time in critical oblivion, Stevie returned to *ex cathedra* applause in the Sixties, both as a poet and as a performer. But the pundits were outshouted by the public. Her little-girl act was a big hit on the stage, where, once again, she knew precisely what she was up to. At any poetry reading in which she participated, she was the undisputed star turn. Not drowning but waving, she took her curtain calls like Joan Sutherland. Yet there is no reason to doubt that her life was desperate to the end.

> Why do I think of Death as a friend?
> It is because he is a scatterer
> He scatters the human frame
> The nerviness and the great pain

7

Throws it on the fresh fresh air
And now it is nowhere
Only sweet Death does this . . .

Her poems, if they were pills to purge melancholy, did not work for her. The best of them, however, work like charms for everyone else. Barbera and McBrien were right to go in search of her. It was worth the legwork and the long stakeout. Stevie Smith is a rare bird, a Maltese falcon. English literature in the modern age, crushed by the amount of official attention paid to it, needs her strangeness, the throwaway artistry that takes every trick, the technique there is no point in analysing because you would have to go on analysing it for ever. In life, she could be a pain in the neck even to those who loved her. Her selfishness was a trial. She would heist the salmon out of the sandwiches and leave the bread to be eaten by others. Even in her work, she can be so fey that the skin crawls. But when she is in form she can deconstruct literature in the only way that counts – by constructing something that feels as if it had just flown together, except you can't take it apart.

New Yorker
28 September, 1987

Somewhere becoming rain

(Philip Larkin, *Collected Poems*, edited by Anthony Thwaite,
Faber, 1988)

A T FIRST glance, the publication in the United States
of Philip Larkin's *Collected Poems* looks like a long shot.
While he lived, Larkin never crossed the Atlantic. Unlike
some other British poets, he was genuinely indifferent to his
American reputation. His bailiwick was England. Larkin
was so English that he didn't even care much about Britain, and he rarely mentioned it. Even within England,
he travelled little. He spent most of his adult life at the
University of Hull, as its chief librarian. A trip to London
was an event. When he was there, he resolutely declined to
promote his reputation. He guarded it but would permit no
hype.

Though Larkin's diffidence was partly a pose, his
reticence was authentic. At no point did he announce
that he had built a better mousetrap. The world had to
prove it by beating a path to his door. The process took
time, but was inexorable, and by now, only three years
after his death, at the age of sixty-three, it has reached a
kind of apotheosis. On the British bestseller lists, Larkin's
Collected Poems was up there for months at a stretch,
along with Stephen Hawking's *A Brief History of Time* and
Salman Rushdie's *The Satanic Verses*. In Larkin's case, this
extraordinary level of attention was reached without either
general relativity's having to be reconciled with quantum
mechanics or the Ayatollah Khomeini's being required to
pronounce anathema. The evidence suggests that Larkin's
poetry, from a standing start, gets to everyone capable of
being got to. One's tender concern that it should survive
the perilous journey across the sea is therefore perhaps

9

misplaced. A mission like this might have no more need of a fighter escort than pollen on the wind.

The size of the volume is misleading. Its meticulous editor, Anthony Thwaite – himself a poet of high reputation – has included poems that Larkin finished but did not publish, and poems that he did not even finish. Though tactfully carried out, this editorial inclusiveness is not beyond cavil. What was elliptically concentrated has become more fully understandable, but whether Larkin benefits from being more fully understood is a poser. Eugenio Montale, in many ways a comparable figure, was, it might be recalled, properly afraid of what he called 'too much light'.

During his lifetime, Larkin published only three mature collections of verse, and they were all as thin as blades. *The Less Deceived* (1955), *The Whitsun Weddings* (1964), and *High Windows* (1974) combined to a thickness barely half that of the *Collected Poems*. Larkin also published, in 1966, a new edition of his early, immature collection, *The North Ship*, which had first come out in 1945. He took care, by supplying the reissue with a deprecatory introduction, to keep it clearly separate from the poems that he regarded as being written in his own voice.

The voice was unmistakable. It made misery beautiful. One of Larkin's few even halfway carefree poems is 'For Sydney Bechet', from *The Whitsun Weddings*. Yet the impact that Larkin said Bechet made on him was exactly the impact that Larkin made on readers coming to him for the first time:

> On me your voice falls as they say love should,
> Like an enormous yes.

What made the paradox delicious was the scrupulousness of its expression. There could be no doubt that Larkin's outlook on life added up to an enormous no, but pessimism had been given a saving grace. Larkin described an England changing in ways he didn't like. He described himself ageing in ways he didn't like. The empire had shrunk to a few islands, his personal history to a set of missed opportunities. Yet his desperate position, which ought logically to have been a licence for incoherence, was expressed with such linguistic fastidiousness on the one hand, and such lyrical enchantment on the other, that the question arose of whether he had not at least partly cultivated that view in order to get those results. Larkin once told an interviewer, 'Deprivation for me is what daffodils were for Wordsworth.'

In the three essential volumes, the balanced triad of Larkin's achievement, all the poems are poised vibrantly in the force field of tension between his profound personal hopelessness and the assured command of their carrying out. Perfectly designed, tightly integrated, making the feeling of falling apart fit together, they release, from their compressed but always strictly parsable syntax, sudden phrases of ravishing beauty, as the river in Dante's Paradise suggests by giving off sparks that light is what it is made of.

These irresistible fragments are everyone's way into Larkin's work. They are the first satisfaction his poetry offers. There are other and deeper satisfactions, but it was his quotability that gave Larkin the biggest cultural impact on the British reading public since Auden – and over a greater social range. Lines by Larkin are the common property of everyone in Britain who reads seriously at all – a state of affairs which has not obtained since the time of Tennyson. Phrases, whole lines, and sometimes whole stanzas can be heard at the dinner-table.

There is an evening coming in
Across the fields, one never seen before,
That lights no lamps . . .

Only one ship is seeking us, a black-
Sailed unfamiliar, towing at her back
A huge and birdless silence. In her wake
No waters breed or break . . .

Now, helpless in the hollow of

An unarmorial age, a trough
Of smoke in slow suspended skeins
Above their scrap of history,
Only an attitude remains . . .

And as the tightened brakes took hold, there swelled
A sense of falling, like an arrow-shower
Sent out of sight, somewhere becoming rain . . .

How distant, the departure of young men
Down valleys, or watching
The green shore past the salt-white cordage
Rising and falling . . .

Steep beach, blue water, towels, red bathing caps,
The small hushed waves' repeated fresh collapse
Up the warm yellow sand, and further off
A white steamer stuck in the afternoon . . .

Later, the square is empty: a big sky
Drains down the estuary like the bed
Of a gold river . . .

At death, you break up: the bits that were you
Start speeding away from each other for ever
With no one to see . . .

Rather than words comes the thought of
   high windows:
The sun-comprehending glass,
And beyond it, the deep blue air, that shows
Nothing, and is nowhere, and is endless.

Drawn in by the subtle gravity beam of such bewitch-
ment, the reader becomes involved for the rest of his life
in Larkin's doomed but unfailingly dignified struggle to
reconcile the golden light in the high windows with the
endlessness it comes from. His sense of inadequacy, his fear
of death are in every poem. His poems could not be more
personal. But, equally, they could not be more universal.
Seeing the world as the hungry and thirsty see food and
drink, he describes it for the benefit of those who are at

home in it, their senses dulled by satiation. The reader asks: How can a man who feels like this bear to live at all?

> Life is first boredom, then fear.
> Whether or not we use it, it goes,
> And leaves what something hidden from us chose,
> And age, and then the only end of age.

But the reader gets an answer: There are duties that annul nihilism, satisfactions beyond dissatisfaction, and, above all, the miracle of continuity. Larkin's own question about what life is worth if we have to lose it he answers with the contrary question, about what life would amount to if it didn't go on without us. Awkward at the seaside, ordinary people know better in their bones than the poet among his books:

> The white steamer has gone. Like breathed-on glass
> The sunlight has turned milky. If the worst
> Of flawless weather is our falling short,
> It may be that through habit these do best,
> Coming to water clumsily undressed
> Yearly; teaching their children by a sort
> Of clowning; helping the old, too, as they ought.

Just as Larkin's resolutely prosaic organisation of a poem is its passport to the poetic, so his insight into himself is his window on the world. He is the least solipsistic of artists. Unfortunately, this fact has now become less clear. Too much light has been shed. Of the poems previously unpublished in book form, a few are among his greatest achievements, many more one would not now want to be without, and all are good to have. But all the poems he didn't publish have been put in chronological order of composition along with those he did publish, instead of being given a separate section of their own. There is plenty of editorial apparatus to tell you how the original slim volumes were made up, but the strategic economy of their initial design has been lost.

All three of the original volumes start and end with the clean, dramatic decisiveness of a curtain going up and coming down again. The cast is not loitering in the auditorium beforehand. Nor is it to be found hanging out in the car park afterward. *The Less Deceived* starts with 'Lines on a Young Lady's Photograph Album', which laments a lost love but with no confessions of the poet's personal inadequacy. It ends with 'At Grass', which is not about him but about horses: a bugle call at sunset.

> Only the groom, and the groom's boy,
> With bridles in the evening come.

Similarly, *The Whitsun Weddings* starts and ends without a mention of the author. The first poem, 'Here', is an induction into 'the surprise of a large town' that sounds as if it might be Hull. No one who sounds as if he might be Larkin puts in an appearance. Instead, other people do, whose 'removed lives/loneliness clarifies'. The last poem in the book, 'An Arundel Tomb', is an elegy written in a church crypt which is as sonorous as Gray's written in a churchyard, and no more petulant: that things pass is a fact made majestic, if not welcome.

As for *High Windows*, the last collection published while he was alive, it may contain, in 'The Building', his single most terror-stricken – and, indeed, terrifying – personal outcry against the intractable fact of death, but it begins and ends with the author well in the background. 'To the Sea', the opening poem, the one in which the white steamer so transfixingly gets stuck in the afternoon, is his most thoroughgoing celebration of the element that he said he would incorporate into his religion if he only had one: water. 'The Explosion' closes the book with a heroic vision of dead coal miners which could be called a hymn to immortality if it did not come from a pen that devoted so much effort to pointing out that mortality really does mean what it says.

These two poems, 'To the Sea' and 'The Explosion', which in *High Windows* are separated by the whole length of a short but weighty book, can be taken together as a case in point, because, as the chronological arrangement of the *Collected Poems* now reveals, they were written together, or almost. The first is dated October, 1969, and the second is dated January 5, 1970. Between them in *High Windows* come poems dated anything from five years earlier to three years later. This is only one instance, unusually striking but typical rather than exceptional, of how Larkin moved poems around through compositional time so that they would make in emotional space the kind of sense he wanted, and not another kind. Though there were poems he left out of *The Less Deceived* and put into *The Whitsun Weddings*, it would be overbold to assume that any poem, no matter how fully achieved, that he wrote before *High Windows* but did not publish in it would have found a context later – or even earlier if he had been less cautious. Anthony Thwaite goes some way toward assuming exactly that – or, at any rate, suggesting it – when he says that Larkin had been stung by early refusals and had later on repressed excellent poems even when his friends urged him to publish them. Some of these poems, as we now see, were indeed excellent, but if a man is so careful to arrange his works in a certain order it is probably wiser to assume that when he subtracts something he is adding to the arrangement.

Toward the end of his life, in the years after *High Windows*, Larkin famously dried up. Poems came seldom. Some of those that did come equalled his best, and 'Aubade' was among his greatest. Larkin thought highly enough of it himself to send it out in pamphlet form to his friends and acquaintances, and they were quickly on the telephone to one another quoting phrases and lines from it. Soon it was stanzas, and in London there is at least one illustrious playwright who won't go home from a dinner party before he has found an excuse to recite the whole thing.

> This is a special way of being afraid
> No trick dispels. Religion used to try,
> That vast moth-eaten musical brocade

Created to pretend we never die,
And specious stuff that says *No rational being*
Can fear a thing it will not feel, not seeing
That this is what we fear – no sight, no sound,
No touch or taste or smell, nothing to think with,
Nothing to love or link with,
The anaesthetic from which none come round . . .

Had Larkin lived longer, there would eventually have had to be one more slim volume, even if slimmer than slim. But that any of the earlier suppressed poems would have gone into it seems very unlikely. The better they are, the better must have been his reasons for holding them back. Admittedly, the fact that he did not destroy them is some evidence that he was not averse to their being published after his death. As a seasoned campaigner for the preservation of British holograph manuscripts – he operated on the principle that papers bought by American universities were lost to civilisation – he obviously thought that his own archive should be kept safe. But the question of *how* the suppressed poems should be published has now been answered: Some other way than this. Arguments for how good they are miss the point, because it is not their weakness that is inimical to his total effect; it is their strength. There are hemistiches as riveting as anything he ever made public.

Dead leaves desert in thousands . . .

He wrote that in 1953 and sat on it for more than thirty years. What other poet would not have got it into print somehow? The two first lines of a short poem called 'Pigeons', written in 1957, are a paradigm distillation of his characteristic urban pastoralism:

On shallow slates the pigeons shift together,
Backing against a thin rain from the west . . .

Even more remarkable, there were whole big poems so

16

close to being fully realised that to call them unfinished sounds like effrontery. Not only would Larkin never let a flawed poem through for the sake of its strong phrasing; he would sideline a strong poem because of a single flaw. But 'Letter to a Friend about Girls', written in 1959, has nothing frail about it except his final indecision about whether Horatio is writing to Hamlet or Hamlet to Horatio. The writer complains that the addressee gets all the best girls without having to think about it, while he, the writer, gets, if any, only the ones he doesn't really want, and that after a long struggle.

> After comparing lives with you for years
> I see how I've been losing: all the while
> I've met a different gauge of girl from yours . . .

A brilliantly witty extended conceit, full of the scatalogical moral observation that Larkin and his friend Kingsley Amis jointly brought back from conversation into the literature from which it had been banished, the poem has already become incorporated into the Larkin canon that people quote to one another. So have parts of 'The Dance', which would probably have been his longest single poem if he had ever finished it. The story of an awkward, put-upon, recognisably Larkin-like lonely man failing to get together with a beautiful woman even though she seems to be welcoming his attentions, the poem could logically have been completed only by becoming a third novel to set beside *Jill* and *A Girl in Winter*. (Actually, the novel had already been written, by Kingsley Amis, and was called *Lucky Jim*.) But there might have been a better reason for abandoning the poem. Like the Horatio poem and many of the other poems that were held back, 'The Dance' is decisive about what Larkin otherwise preferred to leave indeterminate. 'Love Again', written in 1979, at the beginning of the arid last phase in which the poems that came to him seem more like bouts of fever than like showers of rain, states the theme with painful clarity.

Love again: wanking at ten past three
(Surely he's taken her home by now?),
The bedroom hot as a bakery . . .

What hurts, though, isn't the vocabulary. When Larkin speaks of 'Someone else feeling her breasts and cunt', he isn't speaking with untypical bluntness: though unfalteringly well judged, his tonal range always leaves room for foul language – shock effects are among his favourites. The pain at this point comes from the fact that it is so obviously Larkin talking. This time, the voice isn't coming through a persona: it's the man himself, only at his least complex, and therefore least individual. In his oeuvre, as selected and arranged by himself, there is a dialogue going on, a balancing of forces between perfection of the life and of the work – a classic conflict for which Larkin offers us a resolution second in its richness only to the later poems of Yeats. In much of the previously suppressed poetry, the dialogue collapses into a monologue. The man who has, at least in part, chosen his despair, or who, at any rate, strives to convince himself that he has, is usurped by the man who has no choice. The second man might well be thought of as the real man, but one of the effects of Larkin's work is to make us realise that beyond the supposed bedrock reality of individual happiness or unhappiness there is a social reality of creative fulfilment, or, failing that, of public duties faithfully carried out.

Larkin, in his unchecked personal despair, is a sacrificial goat with the sexual outlook of a stud bull. He thinks, and sometimes speaks, like a Robert Crumb character who has never recovered from being beaten up by a girl in the third grade. The best guess, and the least patronising as well, is that Larkin held these poems back because he thought them self-indulgent – too private to be proportionate. One of the consolations that Larkin's work offers us is that we can be unhappy without giving in, without letting our wish to be off the hook ('Beneath it all, desire of oblivion runs') wipe out our lives ('the million-petalled flower/Of being here'). The ordering of the individual volumes was clearly meant to preserve this balance, which the inclusion of even a few more of the suppressed poems would have tipped.

In the *Collected Poems*, that hard-fought-for poise is quite gone. Larkin now speaks a good deal less for us all, and a good deal more for himself, than was his plain wish. That the self, the sad, dithering personal condition from which all his triumphantly assured work sprang, is now more comprehensively on view is not really a full compensation, except, perhaps, to those who aren't comfortable with an idol unless its head is made from the same clay as its feet.

On the other hand, to be given, in whatever order, all these marvellous poems that were for so long unseen is a bonus for which only a dolt would be ungrateful. Schnabel said that Beethoven's late piano sonatas were music better than could be played. Larkin's best poems are poetry better than can be said, but sayability they sumptuously offer. Larkin demands to be read aloud. His big, intricately formed stanzas, often bridging from one to the next, defeat the single breath but always invite it. As you read, the ideal human voice speaks in your head. It isn't his: as his gramophone records prove, he sounded like someone who expects to be interrupted. It isn't yours, either. It's ours. Larkin had the gift of reuniting poetry at its most artful with ordinary speech at its most unstudied – at its least literary. Though a scholar to the roots, he was not being perverse when he posed as a simple man. He thought that art should be self-sufficient. He was disturbed by the way literary studies had crowded out literature. But none of this means that he was simplistic. Though superficially a reactionary crusader against modernism, a sort of latter-day, one-man Council of Trent, he knew exactly when to leave something unexplained.

The process of explaining him will be hard to stop now that this book is available. It is still, however, a tremendous book, and, finally, despite all the candour it apparently offers, the mystery will be preserved for any reader acute enough to sense the depth under the clarity. Pushkin said that everything was on his agenda, even the disasters. Larkin knew about himself. In private hours of anguish, he commiserated with himself. But he was an artist, and that meant he was everyone; and what made him a genius was the effort and resource he brought to bear in order to meet his superior responsibility.

Larkin went to hell, but not in a handcart. From his desolation he built masterpieces, and he was increasingly disinclined to settle for anything less. About twenty years ago in Britain, it became fashionable to say that all the poetic excitement was in America. Though things look less that way now, there is no need to be just as silly in the opposite direction. The English-speaking world is a unity. Britain and the United States might have difficulty absorbing each other's poetry, but most people have difficulty with poetry anyway. In Britain, Larkin shortened the distance between the people and poetry by doing nothing for his career and everything to compose artifacts that would have an independent, memorable life apart from himself. There is no inherent reason that the American reader, or any other English-speaking reader, should not be able to appreciate the results.

Art, if it knows how to wait, wins out. Larkin had patience. For him, poetry was a life sentence. He set happiness aside to make room for it. And if it turns out that he had no control over where his misery came from, doesn't that mean that he had even more control than we thought over where it went to? Art is no less real for being artifice. The moment of truth must be prepared for. 'Nothing to love or link with,' wrote Larkin when he was fifty-five. 'Nothing to catch or claim,' he wrote when he was twenty-four, in a poem that only now sees the light. It was as if the death he feared to the end he had embraced at the start, just so as to raise the stakes.

New Yorker
17 July, 1989

Last Will and Testament

(*The Drowned and the Saved* by Primo Levi, translated from the Italian by Raymond Rosenthal, Michael Joseph, 1988)

Pᴿᴵᴹᴼ ʟᴇᴠɪ's last book, *The Drowned and the Saved* – published in Italy before he committed suicide – is the condensed, poised summation of all his written work, which includes novels, memoirs, poems, short stories, and critical articles. All his books dealt more or less directly with the disastrous historical earthquake of which the great crimes of Nazi Germany constitute the epicentre, and on whose shifting ground we who are alive still stand. None of the books are less than substantial and some of them are masterpieces, but they could all, at a pinch, be replaced by this one, which compresses what they evoke into a prose argument of unprecedented cogency and force. If the unending tragedy of the Holocaust can ever be said to make sense, then it does so in these pages. The book has not been as well translated as one could wish – Levi's supreme mastery of prose is reduced to something merely impressive – but its status as an indispensable guidebook to the infernal cellars of the age we live in is beyond doubt from the first chapter.

That we need guidance is one of the things Levi was always insistent about. He insisted quietly, but on that point he never let up. In a tough joke on himself, he acknowledged his kinship with the Ancient Mariner – the epigraph of this book is from Coleridge's poem – but he didn't apologise for telling his ghastly tale. The mind will reject this kind of knowledge if it can. Such ignorance doesn't even have to be willed. It is a protective mechanism. Levi was in no doubt that this mechanism needs to be overridden. Not knowing about what didn't suit them was how people let the whole thing happen in the first place.

A powerful aid to not knowing was the scale of the horror, hard to imagine even if you were there. The SS taunted the doomed with the assurance that after it was all over, nobody left alive would be able to credit what had happened to the dead, so there would be nothing to mark their passing – not even a memory. Levi's argument, already a summary, is difficult to summarise further, but if a central tenet can be extracted it would have to do with exactly that – memory. Beyond the evidence, which is by now so mountainous that it can be challenged only by the insane, there is the interpretation of the evidence. To interpret it correctly, even we who are sane have to grasp what things were really like. Levi is trying to make us see something that didn't happen to us as if we remembered it. There are good reasons, I think, for believing that not even Levi could fully succeed in this task. We can't live with his memories, and in the long run it turned out that not even he could. But if he has failed he has done so only to the extent of having been unable to concoct a magic potion, and in the process he has written a classic essay.

In Auschwitz, most of Levi's fellow Italian Jews died quickly. If they spoke no German and were without special skills, nothing could save them from the gas chambers and the ovens. Like most of the deportees from all the other parts of Nazi-occupied Europe, they arrived with small idea of where they were, and died before they could find out. Levi's training as a chemist made him exploitable. The few German words he had picked up in his studies were just enough to convey this fact to the exploiters. In the special camp for useful workers – it is fully described in his first and richest book, *Survival in Auschwitz* – Levi was never far from death, but he survived to write his testimony, in the same way that Solzhenitsyn survived the Gulag, and for the same reason: privilege. If Solzhenitsyn had not been a mathematician, we would probably never have heard of him as a writer. But if Levi had not been a chemist we would certainly never have heard of him as a writer. In the Soviet labour camp, death, however plentiful, was a by-product. The Nazi extermination camp was dedicated exclusively to its manufacture. Luck wasn't enough to bring you through. You had to have an edge on all the others. The proposition sounds pitiless until Levi explains it: 'We, the survivors, are not the true witnesses.' The typical prisoner did not get out alive. Those at the heart of the story had no story.

Shame, according to Levi, is thus the ineluctable legacy of all who lived. Reduced to a bare ego, the victim was under remorseless pressure to ignore the fate of everyone except himself. If he had friends, he and his friends were against the others, at least to the extent of not sharing with them the extra piece of bread that could make the difference between life and death within the conspiratorial circle but if shared outside would not be even a gesture, because everyone would die. During a heatwave, Levi found a few extra mouthfuls of water in a rusty pipe. He shared the bounty only with a close friend. He might have told others about this elixir of life, but he did not. Luckily, his self-reproach, though patently bitter, helps rather than hinders his effort to re-create for us the stricken landscape in which feelings of complicity were inescapable.

One of Levi's several triumphs as a moralist – for once, the word can be used with unmixed approval – is that he has analysed these deep and complicated feelings of inexpungible shame without lapsing into the relativism that would make everyone guilty. If everyone was guilty, then everyone was innocent, and Levi is very certain that his persecutors were not innocent. The Nazis were as guilty as the hell they built. The good citizens who decided not to know were less guilty but still guilty. There were many degrees of guilt among those who were not doing the suffering. Some of them were as innocent as you can be while still being party to a crime. But parties to a crime they all were. The victims of the crime had nothing at all in common with those who planned it or went along with it. The victims who survived, and who were ashamed because they did, were not responsible for their shame, because they were driven to it. Even if they did reprehensible things – in the area of behaviour that Levi calls the Grey Zone – they could reasonably contend that they would never have contemplated such conduct in normal circumstances, from which they had been displaced through no fault of their own.

Levi has no harsh words even for those most terribly contaminated of survivors, the *Sonderkommando* veterans. The few still alive decline to speak. Levi believes that the right to silence of these men, who chose to live at the price of co-operating with the killers, should be respected. He is able to imagine – able, momentarily, to make *us* imagine – that the chance of postponing one's own death was hard to turn down, even at the cost of having to attend closely upon the unspeakable deaths of countless others. Levi manages to sympathise even with the Kapos, not all of whom were sadists, and all of whom wanted to live. Levi has no sympathy for the persecutors, but he is ready to understand them, as long as he is not asked to exonerate them. His patience runs out only when it comes to those who parade their compassion without realising that they are trampling on the memory of the innocent dead. As a writer, Levi always keeps his anger in check, the better to distribute its intensity, but occasionally you sense that he is on the verge of an outburst. One such moment is when he reproves the film director Liliana Cavani, who has offered the opinion 'We are all victims or murderers, and we accept these roles voluntarily.' Faced with this brand of self-indulgent vaporising, Levi expresses just enough contempt to give us an inkling of what his fury would have been like if he had ever let rip. To confuse the murderers with their victims, he says, 'is a moral disease or an aesthetic affectation or a sinister sign of complicity; above all, it is precious service rendered (intentionally or not) to the negators of truth.'

Levi might have written like that all the time if he had wished. But his sense of proportion never let him down. The offence was too great for individual anger to be appropriate. Emerging from his discussion of the Grey Zone of behaviour, in which the survivors, pushed to the edge of the pit, were excusably reduced to base actions that they would not have dreamed of in real life, he goes on to discuss the inexcusably base actions of those engineers of cruelty who made sure that even the millions of victims murdered immediately on arrival would have an education in despair before they died. In a chapter called 'Useless Violence', Levi reminds us that we should not set too much store by the idea that the Nazi extermination programme was, within its demented limits, carried out rationally. Much of the cruelty had no rational explanation whatsoever. No matter how long it took the train to reach the camp, the boxcars were never provided with so much as a bucket. It wasn't that the SS were saving themselves trouble: since the boxcars had to be sent back in reasonable shape to be used again, it would actually have been *less* trouble to provide them with some sort of facility, however crude. There was no reason not to do so except to cause agony. Old people who were already dying in their homes were thrown onto the trains lest they miss out on the death the Nazis had decided was due them, the death with humiliation as a prelude.

You would expect Levi's voice to crack when he writes of such things, but instead it grows calmer. He doesn't profess to fully comprehend what went on in the minds of people who could relish doing such things to their fellow human beings. His tone of voice embodies his reticence. He is not reticent, however, about any commentator who *does* profess to fully understand, without having understood the most elementary facts of the matter. After the protracted and uncertain journey recorded in 'The Reawakening', Levi at last returned to Italy, and there was told that his survival must surely have been the work of Providence: fate had preserved him, a friend said, so that he might testify. In this book Levi characterises that idea as 'monstrous': a big word for him – almost as big as any word he ever uses about the events themselves.

He is firm on the point, but this firmness is only a subdued echo of how he made the same point at the end of the 'October 1944' chapter of *Survival in Auschwitz*, where the prisoner Kuhn, after the terrifying process of selection for the gas chambers has once again passed him by, loudly and personally thanks God. In the earlier book Levi was scornful of Kuhn's selfishness in believing that the Providence that had ignored so many should be concerned to preserve him. ('If I was God, I would spit at Kuhn's prayer.') In this book, the same argument is put no less decisively, but more in sorrow than in anger, as if such folly were ineradicable, a part of being human. Though Levi was never a fatalist, at the end of his life he seems to have been readier to accept that human beings are frail and would prefer to misunderstand these things if given the opportunity. Wonderfully, however, he remained determined not to give them the opportunity. At the very time when he feared that the memory and its meaning might slip from the collective human intelligence and go back into the historic past that we only pretend concerns us, Levi's trust in human reason was at its most profound. Transparent even in its passion, level-headed at the rim of the abyss, the style of his last book is an act of faith.

From the translation, however, you can't always tell. Raymond Rosenthal has mainly done a workmanlike job where something more accomplished was called for, and sometimes he is not even workmanlike. *The Drowned and the Saved* ranks with Nadezhda Mandelstam's *Hope Against Hope* as a testament of the age, but Nadezhda Mandelstam's translator was Max Hayward, whose English was on a par with her Russian. One doesn't want to berate Mr Rosenthal, who has toiled hard, but one might be forgiven for wishing that his editors had noticed when he needed help. If they weren't aware that a paragraph by Levi always flows smoothly as a single rhythmic unit, they should at least have guessed that a sentence by Levi is never nonsense – and when it comes down to detail the translation all too often obscures what Levi took pains to make clear, dulls the impact of his most precisely calculated effects, and puts chaos back into the order he achieved at such cost.

There doesn't seem to have been much editorial

control at all. Punctuation is arbitrary and spellings have been left unchecked. In the original Italian text, Levi left a handful of German words – part of the uniquely ugly vocabulary of Naziism – untranslated, so that they would stand out with suitable incongruity. In this Englished version they are treated the same way, but some of them are misspelled, which might mean either that Mr Rosenthal does not read German or that he does not read proofs, but certainly means that the editors were careless. A *Geheimnisträger* is a bearer of secrets. If *Geheimnisfräger* means anything, it would mean an asker of secrets, which is the opposite of what Levi intended. This kind of literal misprint can happen to anyone at any time and is especially likely to be introduced at the last moment while other errors are being corrected, but another piece of weird German seems to have originated with the translator himself. 'There is an unwritten but iron law, *Zurüchschlagen*: answering blows with blows is an intolerable transgression that can only occur to the mind of a "newcomer", and anyone who commits it must be made an example.' The word should be *zurückschlagen*, with a lower case 'z' because it is not a noun, and a 'k' instead of the first 'h'. Worse, and probably because the word has not been understood, the first comma and the colon have been transposed, thereby neatly reversing the sense. What Levi is saying is that it was against the law to strike back. The English text says that this law was called: to strike back. An important point has been rendered incomprehensible.

The translator's Italian is good enough to make sure that he usually doesn't, when construing from that language, get things backward, but he can get them sidewise with daunting ease, and on several occasions he puts far too much trust in his ear. To render *promiscuità* as 'promiscuity', as he does twice, is, in the context, a howler. Levi didn't mean that people forced to live in a ghetto were tormented by promiscuity. He meant that they were tormented by propinquity. The unintentional suggestion that they were worn out by indiscriminate lovemaking is, in the circumstances, a bad joke. Similarly, the Italian word *evidentemente*, when it means 'obviously', can't be translated as 'evidently', which always implies an element of doubt; that is, means virtually the opposite. 'Also in the certainly much vaster field of the victim one observes a drifting of memory, but here, evidently, fraud is not involved.' Thus a point about which Levi is morally certain is made tentative. Again, the word *comportamenti* is good plain Italian, but 'behaviors' is sociologese: the translator has left room for the reader to suspect that Levi was prone to jargon, when in fact he eschewed it rigorously, out of moral conviction.

Sometimes neglect attains the level of neologism. When Levi says that the daily life of the Third Reich was profoundly *compenetrato* by the Lager system, the word *compenetrato* is hard to translate; 'penetrated' isn't comprehensive enough, but you certainly can't render it as 'compentrated', which looks like a misprint anyway and, even if it had an 'e' between the 'n' and the 't', would still send you straight to the dictionary – and it would have to be a big one. Such a verbal grotesquerie, however, at least has the merit of being easy to spot. More insidious are transpositions of meaning which sound plausible. There are sentences that have, under a troubled surface, an even more troubled depth. 'But it is doubtless that this torment of body and spirit, mythical and Dantesque, was excogitated to prevent the formation of self-defence and active resistance nuclei: the Lager SS were obtuse brutes, not subtle demons.' Here *nuclei di autodifesa o di resistenza attiva*, which could have been translated in the same word order and sounded like good English, has been pointlessly inverted to sound like sociologese; and *escogitato* has been taken straight when it needed, for naturalness, to be turned into some simpler word, such as 'planned' or 'devised'. But you could make these repairs and still leave the deeper damage undisturbed. The word 'doubtless' should be 'doubtful'. Retroactively this becomes clear. The rest of the paragraph eventually tells you that its first sentence is nonsensical. There is the satisfaction of solving a brainteaser. It is an inappropriate pleasure; Levi was not writing *Alice's Adventures in Wonderland*. Having actually

28

been through the looking-glass into the realm of perverted logic, he came back with an urgent commitment to lucidity. Watching his helpers frustrate him in this aim is not pleasant.

Most of these glitches are at the level of vocabulary and grammar. Another inadequacy, though it matters less for the purpose of initial comprehension, has the eventual effect of denying us knowledge of Levi's intimacy with the literary tradition to which he contributed and by which he was sustained. As his book of essays *Other People's Trades* explicitly reveals, Levi was cultivated in the literatures of several languages. But the literature of his own language had cultivated him. He was *compenetrato* with the poetry and prose of his national heritage. In this book he acknowledges quotations from Manzoni and Leopardi, but, like most Italian writers, he assumes that allusions to Dante need not be flagged. It was foolishly confident of the editors of this English edition to assume the same thing.

Levi often echoes Dante. All too frequently, the translator fails to alert us that this is happening. To leave the allusions unexplained is to weaken the central meaning, because they are always functional. A typical instance is in the passage about those Nazis who for ideological reasons had ended up among the prisoners: 'They were disliked by everyone.' The word *spiacenti*, which would not occur in everyday language, is a reference to 'Inferno' III, 63, where it describes those who have been rejected by both God and God's enemies. By the translator's simply rendering what is said, without explaining what is meant, a powerful use of literary allusion has been turned into patty-cake. Still, the sense survives, and there are worse faults in a translator than to be occasionally clueless. It is worse to be careless. Levi may have literally said that he was 'intimately satisfied by the symbolic, incomplete, tendentious, sacred representation in Nuremberg,' but *sacra rappresentazione* means a medieval morality play and can't be used here in its literal form without making Levi sound mystical at the very moment when he is making a point of sounding hard-headed.

In Italy, the school editions of Levi's books are thoroughly annotated – in several cases, by Levi himself. It would have been better if his English-language publishers had waited for the school editions to come out and then had them translated, notes and all. Unfortunately, the world of publishing has its own momentum. One can't complain about there having been so much eagerness to get Levi's books translated, but a side-effect of the haste has been that his achievement, so coherent in his own language, looks fragmented in ours. He has had several translators, of varying competence. His carefully chosen titles have sometimes been mangled in translation – especially by his publishers in the United States, who have on the whole been less sensitive than his publishers in Britain to his delicate touch. *'Se Questo È un Uomo*, called *If This Is a Man* in Britain, in the current United States edition is called *Survival in Auschwitz* – a journalistic come-on that no doubt has its merits as an attention-getter but can't be said to prepare the way for a narrative that dedicates itself to avoiding stock responses. In the UK, the title of *La Tregua* is translated as *The Truce*, which is accurate, but in the United States it appears as *The Reawakening*, which is inaccurate, because the whole point of the book is that Levi's long voyage home was merely a pause between two periods of struggle – one to survive physically and the other to cope mentally. As for his important novel *La Chiave a Stella*, it can only be regretted that his publishers across the Atlantic tried so hard to help him. A *chiave a stella* is indeed a kind of wrench, but it is not a monkey wrench. 'The Monkey Wrench', however, would not have been as awkward a title as the one that the book was given, *The Monkey's Wrench*. To translate 'La Chiave a Stella' literally as 'The Star-Shaped Key' might have been too poetic for Levi – who is always too truly poetic to be enigmatic – but a momentary puzzle would have been better than a lasting blur. Levi's exactitude, after all, is not incidental to him. It's him.

Books have their fortunes. If the transmission of Levi's body of work into our language might have gone better, it could also have gone worse. Clearly, all concerned tried their best. It is impossible to imagine that anyone involved – whether translator, editor, designer, or executive – thought lightly of the task. Presumably, Levi's approval was sought and obtained for those clumsy titles: he could read English, and in the last years of his life he attended evening classes, so that he might learn to speak it more fluently. He was vitally interested in guarding the safe passage of his books to a wider world. Yet the results of the transference – in our language, at any rate – are less than wholly satisfactory. Thus we are given yet further evidence that the declension that Levi said he most feared – the way the truth 'slides fatally toward simplification and stereotype, a trend against which I would like here to erect a dike' – is very hard to stem.

How worried should we be about this tendency? Obviously, we should be very worried. But in what *way* should we be worried? The answer to that, I think, is not so readily forthcoming. Most of us choose our friends according to whether or not they understand these matters – or, at any rate, we decline to keep any friends who don't. We are already worried, and might even protest, if pushed to it, that we are worried enough – that if we were any more worried we would get nothing done, and civilisation would collapse anyway. What we are really worried about is all those people who *aren't* worried, especially the young. We assume, along with Santayana, that those who cannot remember the past are condemned to repeat it. Anything written or filmed about the Holocaust – any essay, play, novel, film documentary, or television drama, from this brilliant book by Levi all the way down to the poor, stumbling, and execrated miniseries *Holocaust* itself – is informed by that assumption. Critical reaction to any such treatment of the Holocaust is governed by that same assumption. When it is argued that a rendition of the experience must be faithful to the experience, and that the effectiveness of the rendition will be proportionate to the fidelity, the argument is based on that same assumption. An assumption, however, is all it is. Hard-bitten on the face of it, on closer examination it looks like wishful thinking.

It is undoubtedly true that some people who cannot remember the past are condemned to repeat it. But some people who can't remember the past aren't. More disturbingly, many of those who can remember the past are condemned to repeat it anyway. Plenty of people who remembered the past were sent to die in the extermination camps. Their knowledge availed them nothing, because events were out of their control. One of the unfortunate side-effects of studying German culture up to 1933, and the even richer Austrian culture up to 1938, is the depression induced by the gradual discovery of just how cultivated the two main German-speaking countries were. It didn't help a bit. The idea that the widespread study of history among its intellectual élite will make a nation-state behave better is a pious wish. Whether in the household or in the school playground, ethics are transmitted at a far more basic level than that of learning, which must be pursued for its own sake: learning is not utilitarian, even when – especially when – we most fervently want it to be.

We should face the possibility that written learning, even in the unusually affecting form of an essay like *The Drowned and the Saved*, can be transmitted intact only between members of an intelligentsia already in possession of the salient facts. Clearly, the quality of written speculative discussion will influence the quality of artistic treatments of the subject, in whatever form they may be expressed. Here again, however, we should face the possibility that it might not necessarily be the artistic work of highest quality which influences the public. From Alain Resnais's breathtaking short film *Nuit et Brouillard*, of 1956, to the recent documentary *Shoah*, most of the screen treatments of the fate of the European Jews have been considered by those who know something about the subject to have spread at least a modicum of enlightenment, if only in the form of a useful myth. The exception was the aforementioned American miniseries *Holocaust*, which, although it won a few prizes, also received a worldwide pasting – especially from those critics who saw it in the United States, where it was punctuated by commercials. Even in Britain, where I saw it, any critic who found merit in it was likely to be told that he was insensitive to the subject. But whether those of us who had a good word to say for *Holocaust* were being as crass as it was crude is beside the point here. The point is that it was *Holocaust*, out of all these productions, that had the direct, verifiable historic effect. Just before the miniseries was screened in West Germany, a statute of limitations on Nazi crimes was about to come into effect. After the miniseries was screened, the statute was rescinded. Public opinion had been decisive. It could be said that this was a very late stage for the German public to get wise. It could even be said that if it took a melodrama like *Holocaust* to wake it up, then it was best left sleeping. But it couldn't be denied that a clumsy story had broken through barriers of unawareness that more sophisticated assaults had not penetrated.

Not just of Germany but of all other countries it was, of course, true that the wider public hadn't seen the more sophisticated efforts, so there was no comparison. But this merely proved that if the wider public is to be reached the message has to be popularised. Whether popularised necessarily means vulgarised is the obvious question, to which the answer, however reluctantly given, surely has to be yes. If the *mobile vulgus* is what you want to reach, then there is no virtue in constructing something too oblique for its members to be attracted by, or, if they are attracted, to understand. The more you insist that the event's implications are endless, and the more you pronounce yourself worried that the event's implications somehow haven't been taken in by the general run of humanity, the more you must be committed to some process of reduction. The trick is to popularise without traducing, to simplify without distorting – to vulgarise without violating. At its best, this process will be a distillation, but it is hard to see how dilution can be avoided for long. And, indeed, there are good reasons for supposing that any effort, even the best, to convey the importance of this subject is bound to render it less than it was. Arthur Miller's television film 'Playing for Time' was rightly praised. The performances of Jane Alexander and Vanessa Redgrave were on a par with Meryl Streep's in *Holocaust*, with the difference that Miss Alexander and Miss Redgrave were working with a screenplay that was content to evoke by suggestion what it could not show without cosmeticising. Nothing was shirked except one thing. Though the story about the two brave lovers who escaped was a true one, it was not true that after recapture they died facing each other with one last look of love. The two recaptured runaways are given a private shared moment on the point of death, as if, though their fate was sealed, they could to some extent choose the manner of it. It is a brilliantly dramatic scene. But it is dramatic licence. In reality, there was no choice. In *The Drowned and the Saved* Levi tells what really happened to the two who fled. The Nazis did not allow them any last beautiful moment. Only a work of art can arrange that – and, of course, we want it to, we demand it. It is hard to see how, against this demand to give the meaningless meaning, the full facts, in all their dreadful emptiness, can prevail. We will always look for consolation, and will always need to be talked out of it.

Levi tried to talk us out of it. There is no reason to believe he gave up on the task, because there is no reason to believe he thought that it could ever be fully accomplished in the first place. If we think he died of disappointment, we mistake him, and underestimate the frightfulness he was telling us about. Writing about Tamburlaine, Burckhardt said there were some episodes of history so evil that they weren't even of any use in defining the good: they were simply a dead loss. For all his tough-mindedness about erstwhile horrors, Burckhardt had no inkling that there were more to come. When they came, they were worse. For Burckhardt, the slaughterhouse happened in history: he was able to look back on it with a steady gaze. For Levi, it was life itself. The shock was never over, the suffering was never alleviated. The reason for his suicide, so bewildering at the time, is now, in retrospect, not so hard

34

to guess. In the first chapter of this book he quotes his friend Jean Améry, who was tortured by the Gestapo and committed suicide more than thirty years later: 'Anyone who has been tortured remains tortured.' Levi's admirable sanity might have been produced in part by his dreadful memories, but it was maintained in spite of them. A fit of depression induced by some minor surgery was enough to open the way out which only a continuous act of will had enabled him to keep closed. His style to the end – and, on the evidence of this last book, even more at the end than at the beginning – had the mighty imperturbability of Tacitus, who wrote the truth as though it were worth telling even if there was nobody to listen and no prospect of liberty's being restored. But if Schopenhauer was right to call style the physiognomy of the soul, nevertheless the soul's face has a body, and in Levi's case the body had been injured. Once again, the urge for consolation can lead us astray. We would like to think that in time any pain can be absorbed, rationalised, given a place. But gratuitous violence is not like childbirth; it serves no purpose, and refuses to be forgotten.

Levi's admirers can be excused if they find it more comforting to be appalled by his demise than to admit how they had been lulled by the example of his sweet reason into believing that what he had been through helped to make him a great writer, and that the catastrophe therefore had that much to be said for it, if no more. But part of his greatness as a writer was to warn us against drawing up a phony balance sheet. The idea that it takes extreme experience to produce great literature should never be left unexamined. The great literature that arises from extreme experience covers a very narrow band, and does so at the cost of bleaching out almost the whole of life – the everyday world that enjoys, in Nadezhda Mandelstam's great phrase, 'the privilege of ordinary heartbreaks'. Catastrophes like the Holocaust – and if it is argued that there have been no catastrophes quite like the Holocaust it can't usefully be argued that there won't be – have no redeeming features. Any good that comes out of them belongs not to them but to the world they try to wreck. Our only legitimate consolation is that, although they loom large in the long perspectives of history, history would have no long perspectives if human beings were not, in the aggregate, more creative than destructive. But the mass slaughter of the innocent is not a civics lesson. It involves us all, except that some of us were lucky enough not to be there. The best reason for trying to lead a fruitful life is that we are living on borrowed time, and the best reason to admire Primo Levi's magnificent last book is that he makes this so clear.

New Yorker
23 May, 1988

Galway Kinnell's Great Poem

T HE BEST Hitchcock film was directed by someone else. *Charade* would not be as good as it is if Hitchcock had not developed the genre it epitomises, but Hitchcock could never have created a film so meticulous, plausible, sensitive, light-footed and funny. It took Stanley Donen to do that: temporarily Hitchcock's student, he emerged as his master. Similarly Galway Kinnell's great poem *The Avenue Bearing the Initial of Christ Into the New World* is the long Ezra Pound poem that Pound himself could never have written. It could not have been written without Pound's *Cantos* as a point of departure, but it is so much more human, humane and sheerly poetic that you realise why Pound's emphasis on technique and language, fruitful to others, was barren for himself. A poetic gift will include those things – or anyway the capacity for them – but finally there is an element of personality which brings them to their full potential, and only as a means to an end. With more on his mind than Pound and fewer bees in his bonnet, Kinnell could actually do what Pound spent too much of his time teaching. Pound went on and on about making you see, but the cold truth is that in the *Cantos* there are not many moments that light up. Kinnell's poem has got them like stars in heaven. It is almost unfair.

> Banking the same corner
> A pigeon coasts 5th Street in shadows,
> Looks for altitude, surmounts the rims of buildings,
> And turns white.

Pound *wanted* to sound like that, but found it hard. He made it hard for himself. He was always looking for his vision of history in the way he said things. Kinnell, for the stretch of his own much shorter very long poem, has a vision of history that comes from history. The *Cantos*, the twentieth-century version of Casaubon's 'Key to All the Mythologies' from *Middlemarch*, ranges through all time and all space looking for a pattern, tracing specious lines of connection in which Pound progressively entangles himself, until finally he hangs mummified with only his mouth moving, unable to explain even his own era, a nut for politics whose political role was to be the kind of Fascist that real Fascists found naïve. Kinnell's poem, moving only in the region of New York's Avenue C at the end of World War II, is sustained throughout by historical resonance – the very quality which Pound, yearning to achieve it, always dissipated in advance with his demented certainties.

Along and around Avenue C, in the lower East Side, flows the whole rich experience of immigrant America and its relationship to the terrible fate of modern Europe. Blacks and Puerto Ricans and Jews and Ukrainians toil in uneasy proximity but at least they are alive and there is a law. Only the animals and the fish are massacred. An official, empty letter of condolence from a concentration camp front office to a victim's family is quoted while a Jewish fishmonger guts the catch. It is the sort of effect which Pound, exalting it with the name of juxtaposition, practised like a bad journalist. In Kinnell's poem it attains true complexity, principally because he has the negative capability – the sanity – to let his audience do the interpreting, from their common knowledge.

Pound had a theory about the Jews. Kinnell knew what theories like that led to and presumed that his readers knew too. *The Avenue Bearing the Initial of Christ Into the New World* was one of the first, and remains one of the few, adequate works of art devoted to the Holocaust. The Hassidim walk Avenue C bent over with the weight of their orthodoxy, unassimilable as spacemen. Faced with their intransigence, Kinnell has no easy democratic message. He has the difficult one – the message that America, or at any rate the tip of Manhattan, has something to offer more interesting, and perhaps less threatening, than the prospect of homogeneity. An anti-*Waste Land* that sees the potential creativity in apparent chaos, his poem celebrates diversity, out of which unpredictability comes, a cultural complexity which the artist can only describe.

Helping him to describe it is a gift for evocation which makes it advisable to leave Ezra Pound out of account altogether, since he spent, presumably from preference, little time saying that one thing was like another. *The apparition of these faces in the crowd/leaves on a wet, black bough.* Pound manufactured a few examples like that and then talked about them. Kinnell's less effortful knack for the arc-light metaphor should serve to remind us that the Martian movement must have been landing its flying saucers long before they were first detected.

> We found a cowskull once; we thought it was
> From one of the asses in the Bible, for the sun
> Shone into the holes through which it had seen
> Earth as an endless belt carrying gravel . . .

All the more striking for steering clear of extravagance, that particular coup is from a poem called 'Freedom, New Hampshire'. Nowadays Les Murray studs his poems about country Australia with similar effects, but gets them closer together. Kinnell, in his shorter poems, spaced them out. There was too much else going on. He overstrained his verbs like Lowell, substituted the next-less-intelligible noun throughout the stanza like Wallace Stevens, piled on the archaic diction in a belated tribute to John Crowe Ransom, and above all indulged in rhapsodic apostrophes to the City which recalled Hart Crane the way that Crane had once recalled Walt Whitman.

> And thou, River of Tomorrow, flowing . . .

Like so many poets, especially American poets, who consciously attempt to forge an idiom, Kinnell synthesised the idioms of other poets, many of whom had themselves been up to the same doomed trick. Forging an idiom is forgery, even when dressed up as subservience. Almost everything Kinnell wrote was in agitated, self-conscious homage to someone – William Carlos Williams and Robert Frost loomed like faces on Mount Rushmore – and too often the homage was technical. But Kinnell's proper rhythm and true clarity were there waiting to be brought out at the moment when a strong enough subject turned him away from ambition and towards achievement. *The Avenue Bearing the Initial of Christ Into the New World* is one coup after another, a succession of illuminations like his stunning image of the Avenue's traffic lights going green into the far dusk. Here are the vegetable stalls:

> In the pushcart market on Sunday,
> A crate of lemons discharges light like a battery.
> Icicle-shaped carrots that through black soil
> Wove away like flames in the sun.
> Onions with their shirts ripped seek sunlight
> On green skins. The sun beats
> On beets dirty as boulders in cowfields,
> On turnips pinched and gibbous
> From budging rocks, on embery sweets,
> Peanut-shaped Idahos, shore-pebble Long Islands
>   and Maines,
> On horseradishes still growing weeds on the flat ends,
> Cabbages lying around like sea-green brains
> The skulls have been shucked from . . .

The fish market goes on for several stanzas, at the thematic centre of the poem because the deaths of millions of humans are being called up by the deaths of millions of creatures similarly dumped from one element into another. Admirers of Elizabeth Bishop's precisely observed poems about fish might find it daunting to note how Kinnell sees just as much detail before soaring up and out into extra relevance like Marianne Moore taking off on a broom.

>   . . . two-tone flounders
> After the long contortion of pushing both eyes

To the brown side that they might look up,
Lying brown side down, like a mass laying-on of hands,
Or the oath-taking of an army.

This is magic poetry in the sense that you can't tell
how he does it and can be dissuaded from the idea that
he might be a sorcerer only by the consideration that other
people are billed as magicians too. What finally establishes
Kinnell's *magnum opus* as a successful poem, however, is its
ordinary poetry – ordinary in the sense that it does not
astonish, but does persuade, and even, in the bitter end,
console.

Fishes do not die exactly, it is more
That they go out of themselves, the visible part
Remains the same, there is little pallor,
Only the cataracted eyes which have not shut ever
Must look through the mist which crazed Homer.

Compare this with Hart Crane's famous, wilfully beautiful line about the seal's wide spindrift gaze towards Paradise
and you can see what Kinnell had that Crane hadn't. With
no ordinary language interesting enough to fall back on,
Crane was trying to sound as if he had a lot to say. Kinnell
had a lot to say. All he needed was a theme to contain it. But
for an intelligence whose attention is everywhere, sharp in
all directions, a still point of focus is not easily found. On
Avenue C he found it.

Galway Kinnell wrote his one great tragic, celebratory
poem and never anything quite like it again, possibly
because it is as long as a modern epic can well be even
though everything that matters is included. I think that
an event drove him to begin it, and a particular historic
conjunction allowed him to complete it. In Europe humanity had been brought to the point where it might have lost
faith in its own right to exist; and then America had saved
the world. Later on things were less simple. It was the
right moment; Kinnell was the right man; and a poem
was written which was wonderful against all the odds –

even those formidable odds posed by the very business of being a poet at all, in an age when art has become so self-aware that innocence can be found only at the end of a long search.

1992

The Australian Poetic Republic

Not so far in the future, suggests Ian McEwan in his novel *The Child In Time*, Britain hopes to be self-sufficient in wood. With his novel scarcely embarked on its career, McEwan's wheeze about self-sufficiency in wood has already entered the vocabulary of political debate, as a paradigm case of supposed folly: Thatcherite economics reduced to, or revealed as, absurdity. The idea that Australia can be self-sufficient in poetry ought surely by now to have attained the same status, as an example of how not to think about the relationship of literature and nationhood. But the idea goes on looking more plausible instead of less.

In the first place, Australian poetry, regarded as a totality, becomes steadily more rich. Does it *need* British and American poetry in any more profound sense than Pat Cash needs opponents? In the second place, the British (forget the Americans: this argument has always been about the British) have shown no more understanding, or even simple tolerance, of the Australian achievement in poetry than they did before. Indeed they have shown less. When Evelyn Waugh thought that the very idea of an Australian wine expert was hilarious, Australian wines were already excellent. Now that Auberon Waugh concedes this, do their producers need to feel gratified, or even interested? The endorsement seems as otiose as the condemnation. So why worry about the international status of an Australian poet? Isn't that the very clue to the proven vitality of the arts in Australia – that they have at last stopped caring about anything beyond a local reception?

The above train of thought is not one in which I fully believe, but I believe in its force, so I have tried to present it with some of the rhetorical pageantry which, say, an Australian broadcasting executive would employ if he were telling you why not only his television station but the public itself profits both materially and spiritually from commercials screened only five minutes apart. My own view, which I hope is a sane one and not just wishful thinking, is that Australian literature and the literature of the old world – the old world which, from the Australian viewpoint, includes most of what used to be called the new world – are bound in a permanent relationship, if only because the old world is a world elsewhere, and would have to be invoked even if Australia were truly isolated, or else what would it be isolated from?

But the relationship has not been, and never can be, based on understanding. Britain (because when we talk about the old world we are still talking principally, if not exclusively, of Britain) can't be persuaded, even if it wanted to be, to appreciate Australian poetry in its full wealth. One of the reasons why Australian poetry has attained its full wealth is that it has learned to do without outside appreciation. So really it is vain to carp.

In the early Sixties, the late and much missed British poet-critic Francis Hope pronounced himself unimpressed with an anthology of recent Australian verse. Hope singled out Bruce Dawe for particular disapprobation. So seemingly casual a dismissal was greeted with bitter protests in Australia. As it happens, Hope could not have been more wrong about Dawe, whose originality and solidity should have been apparent to him, especially since Hope himself was an accomplished poet, and no mere onlooker. But suppose Hope had said the right thing: would that have helped Dawe? Isn't it just as likely that such a clear sign of indifference helped arm Dawe for the long struggle – which he has pursued ever since – to please no critical taste except his own? So there is the first thing to say about the uncomprehending British: if an Australian poet truly believes that he is contributing to a self-sufficient national literature, then incomprehension from the British is just what he ought to welcome.

The second thing to say about the uncomprehending

British is that they won't be talked out of their indifference by offering them more evidence. As the Australian poets grow older, the British reviewers stay young, succeeding one another in brief generations. Thus there is always a new wave of implacable young critics ready to greet the ageing Australian poet's collected works when a few copies of its latest, augmented version at last complete the long journey by ship, sent back as ballast in partial recompense for some huge consignment of novels by Margaret Drabble. More than twenty years after Francis Hope uncaringly enraged the Australian literary community, Christopher Reid in the *Observer*, reviewing yet another anthology of Australian verse, said, among other things less fatuous, that if the sample it contained of A. D. Hope's poetry was typical, then he (the reviewer) was glad that he had not read any more of it.

At least one reader thought that this was the most clear-cut possible test case. Reid, already a distinguished poet and critic, was the very kind of young British disestablishmentarian writer who was going to be impressed by Australian poetry if anybody was. A. D. Hope was the poet who was going, if anybody was, to impress him. Among Australian writers of any age, sex or stamp, A. D. Hope was, and remains, the unchallenged heavyweight. We quarrel with him; we wonder why he dislikes Hopkins; some of us can't credit that he finds Furphy amusing; but none of us doubts the magnitude of his achievement in poetry – the schooled yet spontaneous, mandarin yet demotic, vitality and variety of it. And Christopher Reid had never even heard of it. Well then, let's call off the whole deal.

But the deal was never on. The British – meaning those few, few even among the *literati*, who are really involved with poetry – nowadays have barely enough time to be concerned with their own poets. They had time to be concerned with Australian poetry only when there was far less of it. Now that Australia has acquired, if it has, a literature of its own as a going concern, the lingering desire to have the mother country sniff its nappy must perforce be given up. Giving up that desire was in fact a precondition of an indigenous culture emerging at all. Everyone realised that, even those who were worried that an Australian literature left to judge itself might prove short of critical talent. These foresaw a great burgeoning of the second-rate. The first-rate had always been there, its inner strength reinforced by scorn of the indifference from abroad. Douglas Stewart, A. D. Hope, James McAuley, Gwen Harwood and Judith Wright had accomplished something beyond the dreams of their great senior partner Kenneth Slessor. Slessor's splendid isolation had ultimately ceased to be fruitful. For the lack of an Australian literary community, he had dried up – if that phrase fits someone who sought the same solace as his predecessor Christopher Brennan.

But the above-named poets who came to prominence in the 1940s and 1950s not only created their own variously enduring verse, they created, irreversibly, an Australian literary community in which it might be cherished. A. D. Hope alone, even if the others had achieved nothing along those lines, would probably have done enough to make the study of Australian literature not just respectable but unchallengably important. It is essential to note the fact (and to take in its implications) that A. D. Hope's internationalism and cosmopolitanism gave his patriotic concerns their dignity, guaranteeing them against the merest taint of nationalistic fervour. Hope (and from here on, in this survey, the surname stands for the Australian patriarch, not the British prodigy) wasn't just the Pushkin of the emergent Australian literary consciousness in modern times, he was the Belinsky: he was the poet-critic in his most benevolent manifestation. But even though Hope reigns supreme as a poet into old age, he no longer rules as a critic. The forces he helped to release were sure to take their own paths, and one of the paths they took was sure to be nationalistic. Rising with the Whitlam era but lingering long after, a broad school of Australian writing has based itself on the assumption that Australia not only has a history worth bothering about, but that all the history worth bothering about has happened in Australia.

It is only seemingly a paradox that this nationalistic school of writing seems ignorant of the poetic achievement of Hope, Stewart, McAuley, Harwood, Wright and all those other dedicated literary figures who paved the way for it. Nationalism is frequently unhistorical. Awkwardly for those finer spirits who would like to dismiss it in advance, it is also often energetic. Any dispassionate reader browsing along the poetry shelves of a good Australian bookshop at the present time (there is nowadays usually a whole set of shelves, half of them filled with the glossy output of the University of Queensland Press) will find himself jolted by the force of expression of political views which seem to have been written down just as they were felt, with no intervening period of being thought out or even pondered.

Dating as it does from Gough Whitlam's fall, one would call this strain of verse reportage postlapsarian – if not for its innocence, which is prelapsarian, sometimes to the point that you can see the apple leave Eve's hand and re-attach itself to the tree of knowledge. At the moment Alan Wearne is the most prominent exponent of the genre. His long verse novel *Nightmarkets*, first published in 1985, is now out in a large-format Penguin. No less a critic than Chris Wallace-Crabbe, himself the author of poems which have earned their permanent place in the anthologies, has hailed Wearne as a prodigy. Certainly he has a voracity for fact. It is easy to see why Wearne is so well in with the editors of *Scripsi*, who consider *Nightmarkets* a sure-fire bet to become a 'classic of our literature': its author is so solidly, or anyway heavily, in the tradition of Pound, Williams, Zukofsky, Olsen and the yellow pages of the telephone directory. The doings of the author's generation in the bleak years after Whitlam's political demise are treated with a sweep and prolixity which will remind you of John dos Passos if you can forget Gavin Bantock. The urge to make the book poetic, however, has helped to ensure that it is not enough like prose, so as a novel it makes itself absurd, especially in the dialogue, which is stilted without

47

being heightened. 'Haven't you had enough,' Louise cried out, 'from those nasty shrill petticoat prigs of Women Who Want To Be Women?'

This is a mouthful for Louise to cry out. Saddled with the belief that 'credence' and 'credibility' mean the same thing, Wearne is not as well equipped as he might be for the precision he aspires to, but he deserves some points for seeing a gap in the market. Australian writing might not have actually *needed* a Hugh McDiarmid, but after the Dismissal crisis – which did for the Australian intelligentsia roughly what Culloden did for the Scots – there was room for one: all he had to do was set up shop. Wearne's earlier verse novel *Out Here* (first published in 1976, but now released in Britain as a paperback from Bloodaxe) is really far preferable to *Nightmarkets*, if only for being so much shorter. By expanding his scope without increasing the compression of his language, Wearne has lowered the temperature of his work to the level where putative poetry stands revealed as cold rice pudding.

As a chronicle of events, however, *Nightmarkets* is of some interest. The author's urge to mythologise his friends should not be allowed to put the reader off. After all, Les Murray, in a surprising number of his excellent poems, mythologises such crepuscular acquaintances as Bob Ellis, who looms in Murray's work as if he, Ellis, were Marlowe to Murray's Shakespeare. Avowedly pursuing failure with the same determination other men expend on the trail of success, not even Ellis, whose flakily confessional memoirs, *Letters to the Future*, have recently been published in Australia, is quite capable of being entirely uninteresting when recalling the salad days of the poets of his generation. The salads in those days were terrible, and something of their flavour – the lettuce moistened by nothing but beetroot juice, the onions with the same half-life as plutonium – has lingered in Ellis's untreated prose ever since. He has made a career out of complaining about his own capacity to fritter away his talent. Those who have good cause to doubt whether this latter entity actually exists might be apt to dismiss his memoirs sight unseen, but they should be advised that they might in this one case entertain the possibility that Ellis might entertain them. Ellis's prose is so hit-and-miss that he can't even beat his breast without hitting himself in the eye, but his reminiscences are – this reviewer can vouch for it – pungently evocative of an epoch, now thirty years gone, when nobody even *dreamed* of government subsidy, and to declare himself a writer was a serious commitment, even for a clown.

It should hardly need saying that merely to mention Les Murray is to heighten the tone of the conversation. When he is propagandising for an Australian republic, Murray can be as postlapsarian as anybody – he has written poems about the demise of the British Empire which could have come out of the first draft of the script of *Gallipoli* – but usually his language is too scrupulous to allow for anything less than a fully considered view, especially when it is a view about language itself. Murray when young discovered within himself, and without prompting, a sympathy for other languages. Diligent cultivation of this sympathy gave him the right and the wherewithal to argue powerfully, in his maturity, for the autonomy of the Australian vernacular. Murray's views on the subject are put at length in his book of essays *Persistence in Folly* and they are too subtle to be fairly summarised here, but broadly it can be said that he makes a self-possessed national stance plausible without denying – which, of course, most of the postlapsarians emphatically do deny – an intimate and inexorable connection with the outside world.

It is a great relief, while recommending Murray's prose, not to feel obliged any longer to recommend his poetry, for which the battle for international recognition may now be considered won. Probably it could not have been lost. The craze for Martian poetry in Britain might have been specifically calculated to prepare for the advent of an Australian poet who finds that kind of stuff as natural as breathing. Murray's new collection *The Daylight Moon* is about to be published in Australia. No doubt, at the proper time, it will be reviewed at length in these pages, but without jumping the gun it should be

49

permissible to say that an already mature talent now shows signs of maturing further, into the mastery that can leave an effect understated. In 'Bats Ultrasound' the first four lines of the opening stanza are of a Martian bravura that might almost be called routine. The really astonishing effect is in the unastonishing last line.

> Sleeping-bagged in a duplex wing
> with fleas, in rock-cleft or building
> radar bats are darkness in miniature,
> their whole face one tufty crinkled ear
> with weak eyes, fine teeth bare to sing.

'Fine teeth', already a standard phrase in conversation, is quietly brought back to full life. The whole book is alight with Murray's usual dazzle but there is a new depth underneath.

Murray's verse has been published in America and is by now so well known in serious British poetry magazines that his presence rivals that of Peter Porter, except that Murray works the trick without giving up his absence. Speaking, however, as one who participated, if only marginally, in the campaign to get Murray reviewed decently abroad, I feel free to voice a doubt as to whether this victory, any more than any other, escapes the law of unintended consequences. It only takes one Australian poet making it abroad to revive the idea, both at home and abroad, that making it abroad is the thing to do. While growing no less ready to insist that a British audience will find much to enjoy in Murray's poetry, one should acknowledge a sharpening, perhaps atavistic, urge to point out that he gets a lot of his strength from being so involved with what happens in Australia, and that other poets who have not attained escape velocity have not necessarily failed to do so because they lacked the power. It could be that they just liked the gravity.

The question of what precisely the Australian writers have lost or gained by being or not being expatriates has been often discussed without really being debated. Most of the writers followed their feet. Even the brightest ones only followed their noses. In retrospect, however, the truly startling news – never news at the time because it broke so slowly – was about how most of the poets stayed where they were. But nothing should be allowed to detract from Peter Porter's achievement. His poetry is the embodiment of what drives, or ought to drive, the Australian expatriate writer – a centripetal force which pulls the world together. The Australian expatriate critic need not feel guilty about pointing to Porter's *Collected Poems* as the best, as well as the most conveniently available, example of what Australian poetry has to offer the world. Yet the critic *is* bound to feel guilty about what he doesn't point to. Bruce Dawe is of an age with Peter Porter. His poetry is published only in Australia, and then only in his off-puttingly entitled compendium *Sometimes Gladness, Collected Poems 1954–1982*. If the title sounds like Rod McKuen talking, nothing in the book sounds quite like anyone else on earth. Without leaving home, Dawe made a journey into the American language. I remember in the 1950s coming across a poem he wrote about a wrestler called Drop-kick Joe Savoldi. It was clear that Dawe liked the American lilt of that name. It was equally clear that he was not ashamed of liking it. There was no need, Dawe had realised, to go in quest of the golden fleece. The golden fleece would come to him. But it would be made of nylon. Dawe was the first Australian poet to take the measure of the junk media and find the poetry in their pathos. He wrote better about the Vietnam war than any other poet, including American poets; and he could do so because he wrote better about television.

> Say, are those plumed shadows
> Flying Horsemen of the First Air Cavalry Division,
> or Hittites bringing the gospel of iron
> to confound the Egyptians?
> What are we up to now?

Above all, Dawe had the originality to admit the fact – which should have been obvious, but wasn't until he articulated it – that the saturating, penetrating impact on Australian culture wasn't British, it was American. The British influence is mainly political, and can be outgrown, although the wise will be tactful enough to outgrow it gratefully. The American influence, however, must either be dealt with or succumbed to. Dawe dealt with it. His sense of humour helped. His poetry sounds easy – truly funny things always sound easy, and never are – but it represents a feat of strength, because the Australian language was so much smaller than the American that for the first to absorb the second was like a snake swallowing a donkey.

Dawe consciously assimilated an alien idiom. Younger poets have been able to assimilate the world entire, sometimes without using their brains at all. The sons and daughters of the immigrants have grown up with a houseful of connections to the old world, which cheap air travel has put less than twenty-four hours away. Where Australian poetry was once faced with the dilemma of either being parochial if it defended itself or of losing its identity if it went international, the problem has now disappeared, leaving only the threat of drowning in its solution. The University of Queensland Press seems willing to print any poet in Australia who can't find a commercial publisher. By no coincidence, the UQP poets vary wildly in quality. Richard Kelly Tipping, in the preface to his collection *Nearer By Far*, tells us that its contents have been 'chosen from the high pile of certified verbal artefacts resulting from my 24 to 34th years to heaven.' The allusion to Dylan Thomas might not be enough to persuade the reader that Tipping, born in 1949, is impelled by a similar bardic gift, or any other kind of gift except unembarrassable enthusiasm.

> & i am a tender sirloin, bleeding in a tray
> in the refrigerated window of time –

Both in name and style, Tipping sounds as if Osbert Lancaster made him up, but the inexhaustible Thomas Shapcott – the Michael Horovitz of the South Pacific – assures us that 'Tipping is witty'. No such fatal endorsement disfigures the cover of John Blight's *Holiday Sea Sonnets*. Blight was born in 1913 and has spent a lifetime lying so low he has hardly been heard of – an approach to poetry that recalls Ian Fairweather's approach to painting. But if Peter Porter's admiration for Blight sounds excessive, the merest glance at any poem in the book will instantly prove that it is not misplaced. Here is a stranded raft.

> A snap decision of the waves
> has tossed it at high tide across
> the reef.

Punning on a whole phrase is a trick for which Geoffrey Hill has been applauded and the Martians elevated to the status of magicians. It is a crowd-pleasing thing for poetry to do, but for a long time Blight has been doing it far from any crowds at all, and one might almost say that such a knack was fundamental to Australian poetry. One says 'almost' because in Australia, as elsewhere, most of the poets have no verbal characteristics whatsoever. Thomas Shapcott, the demiurge of the UQP phalanx, can't, I think, be said to write poetry in any way that distinguishes it from prose chopped up. But his range of artistic reference is fully extended into space and time, as if Michael Kustow had met Dr Who. Shapcott's latest collection *Travel Dice* reveals, among many other things, that he has been in Belgrade; that he has stood in awe of Piero di Cosimo, Titian and Goya; and that he can't spell Davy Crockett but is willing to try. Like all the UQP poets rolled together only more so, he sees nothing wrong with trying to get it all in. To that end, of course, lack of a specific poetic talent can be a positive help, and if there is no particular gift for prose either then the pen can just fly along, because while not everything looks like a prose sentence, anything can pass for a line of verse.

> Time spat a capsule of saliva.
> It was a plane shining in rare atmosphere.
> Now it has landed.

The UQP enterprise is doing its considerable best to put poetry on an industrial basis, rather like Faber in the UK, and so far with a similar exemption from the sceptical heckle. On the whole it is probably better for poets to think of themselves as industrialists than as artists – it is better for them to think of themselves as almost anything than as artists – but when the hard-nosed, high-productivity, *stakhanovite* attitude towards grinding the stuff out is accompanied with vociferous claims to a government grant, the resulting picture of subsidised careerism is not attractive. Reminders that Australian poets once had to look after themselves, and profited from the solitude, are always useful.

Such aids to memory can be found in the anthologies, where poets not generally acclaimed can be found to have done excellent particular things – i.e., poems. First the poems, and then, in the course of time, the poet: that is the desirable order, which ambition will always try to reverse. In *Australian Poetry 1986*, edited by the invaluable Vivian Smith, Philip Hodgins has a Martians-move-over poem about a dam.

Two ibises stand on the rim like taps.

Mr Hodgins sounds like the sort of poet who is content to wait, both for the right idea and for eventual fame.

In *The Penguin Book of Australian Women Poets* Gwen Harwood is the outstanding example of a poet who has gradually attained the first magnitude in her art without ever having had a perceptible career. She has been a miracle of self-effacement: compared with Harwood, Judith Wright is Anna Akhmatova. In the long term, however, intensity must out. Edited with a lethally po-faced feminist introduction by Susan Hampton and Kate Llewellyn, this anthology is nevertheless a gold mine, mainly because so many intelligent Australian women have written good poems without having had time to be poets. Such, indeed, is one of Harwood's continuing themes, which she discovered

54

early in her precociously accomplished prentice years, and
has gone on elaborating into old age. She was a feminist
of the new school while the old school was still current.
She never needed, however, to raise her voice, which has
always deployed itself in the quiet, effortlessly attention-
getting range between Blossom Dearie seated at the piano
and Mary Stuart kneeling at the block.

> Baby, I'm sick to death,
> But I can't die. You do
> the songs, you've got the breath.
> Give them the old soft shoe.
> Put on a lovely show.
> Put on your wig and go.

All of Harwood's poetry moves and sings with that decep-
tively simple formal elegance. Younger poets – and I do not
exclude Les Murray, who has so forgotten his early stanzaic
neatness that when he now attempts Burnsian metres they
limp as if shot – would do well to wonder how she does
it. A. D. Hope has always praised Harwood as an equal.
Some of us have been too slow to realise the rightness of
that judgment, dazzled as we were by her lack of fame.
Getting the measure of a talent like hers is made easier
by Angus & Robertson's Modern Poets series, which first
devoted one of its Penguin-sized paperbacks to her selected
poems in 1975. These little volumes are the best available
introduction to Australian poetry, which has so expanded
as a field of study that the visitor, with the best will in
the world, might be honestly puzzled about how to find
a way in. One wouldn't want to suggest that all of this
critical busywork, even at its most painfully academic, is
a waste of time. Some of the not-so-modern poets whose
lifetime achievements added up to something too slim for
an A & R Modern Poets volume are still well worth studying, both for their works and for the implications of their
careers, which were often difficult and sometimes heroic.
There Was A Crooked Man, edited by Richard Appleton and
Alex Galloway, is an indispensable volume for anyone who

55

admired Lex Banning's poetry when it was coming out in Sydney in the Fifties. Banning was a spastic, so cruelly stricken that it took him an age to get out a sentence, but when he was holding court in Lorenzini's wine bar he was never heard to say anything that was not worth the long wait. 'Your poem has a sort of irrational logic,' a critic once said to him, adding: 'I suppose that's a bad way of describing it.' Banning's answer took almost a minute to emerge. 'It's a bad way of describing logic.'

Banning was condemned to bohemianism but wanted a normal life. His acutely intelligent verse, little though there is of it, raises all the questions about how urbanity in Australian poetry had to be brought about by an act of will. But there is no use supposing that Banning will be considered more than a minor figure by the outsider who is trying to take a general view of Australian poetry. Larger claims can and have been made for David Campbell. A collection of essays, *A Tribute to David Campbell*, has just come out. Well edited by Harry Heseltine, if vilely set on what must have been a hand press once dropped, with unnecessary violence, to partisans in Yugoslavia, this post-humous *Festschrift* leaves no room for doubt that Campbell's attempt to remain obscure was doomed to failure. He was widely admired, and from his A & R Selected volume you can see why, although it is hard to suppress the suspicion that in his case a small pocketable volume is just the right size, because he was repetitive, and too often content to be dilute. He was a gentleman and an amateur.

The Australian old masters have traditionally been more serious than that. What the old masters now need, and have not got, is a form of publication befitting their stature. To adopt the verb current in French literary circles, they should be Pléiadised. Kenneth Slessor's A & R Modern Poets paperback, for example, gives his essence, but everything it leaves out is essential too. Slessor needs a single-volume Pléiade-style thin-paper Collected Works which would contain his poetry, his light verse, his critical prose and his war diaries. These last are currently available as a single volume (*The War Diaries of Kenneth Slessor*, edited

by Clement Semmler) but it is a hefty, overblown production whose insane initial price ensured its arrival in the
remainder shops by the direct route from the warehouse.
A properly organised national publishing venture would
resolve such anomalies.

Who should be Pléiadised, and who not, would be a
question guaranteed to arouse heated answers, as it does
in France. But the line would not be hard to draw. Everyone knows who the old masters are. Douglas Stewart and
James McAuley both wrote criticism which belongs beside
their poetry in the same book or a companion volume. The
only good reason for not putting out A. D. Hope or Judith
Wright in a standard set straight away is that they are still
productive. That early lonely slog, when the only support
they ever got was from each other, made the Australian
poets of their generation hard to stop with anything less
than armour-piercing ammunition. Ordinary small-arms
fire just bounced off.

Judith Wright's A & R *Selected Poems*, while not to be
foregone, is so far from representing the culmination of
her achievement that it might with more truth be said to
mark the end of her first phase. She has brought out several volumes since, and the fate of the latest one, *Phantom
Dwelling*, exemplifies the condition of the major Australian
poets in the twentieth century. It was published in Britain
in 1985 and sank like a stone, with scarcely a single review,
even an unfavourable one. For things to have been otherwise, there would have had to be justice. But as with any
other product, there is no innate justice in the marketing
and consumption of poetry, where the exporter is without
power unless he has a distribution system on the ground.
The point was put more simply by Talleyrand: he who is
absent is wrong. There were too many home-grown Martians for an offshore Martian to get a look in, even with
an idea like this.

Two women find the square root of a sheet.
That is an ancient dance.

57

For her, such radiant imagery was second nature. She had been at it for fifty years. Judith Wright, like Gwen Harwood, has lived out the full life of the woman poet, which more notorious international names have either cut short by suicide or replaced by a succession of notes threatening that very outcome. It is good for Australia's literature, and for its life in general, that there can be no serious argument about the role of women, which in poetry is at least equal to that of men and can plausibly be thought of as supreme. (Not even Hope has ever brought in a line with the sweet rhythm of Harwood, who can go past you like a gull: you don't hear her until she's gone.) Australian poetry, in this way and in many others, is a very *satisfactory* field of creativity. Whether the world should be told, however, is an open question. Perhaps the world should be left to find out for itself. Australian civilization might do better to retain the element of surprise, so that the visitor who walks off the plane in Sydney hoping to clap eyes on Crocodile Dundee will be appropriately stunned to find that Pavarotti is singing at the Opera House.

There is also the consideration that the Australian expatriate, once the secret is all the way out, will lose his privileged status as a barbarian. It has always been a rewarding role to play. Cavafy evoked an ancient Rome dying of impatience because the barbarians were late. If anything, he understated the case. At present, an Australian expatriate in London or New York has only to mention Proust or Rilke and he is greeted as an avatar, as if Paracelsus had come to town. When Australia is correctly regarded as a nation artistically fertile like any other, and more so than any other nation its size – which it ought to be, considering how free and rich it is – the law of rising expectations will make the expatriate's tent-show a bit less of a sure-fire smash hit. There would also be the grim possibility that the British scholars, critics and reviewers finally *would* start taking Australian poetry seriously, with all the grief, rage, academic apparatus and undignified jockeying for position which that would entail.

A possibility is all it is. By now, achievement can be

relied upon to outrun understanding – an order of events which is practically the definition of a living culture. Like the Australian cities, where the place to go and the thing to do are nowadays always in the next edition of the guide book, Australian poetry is currently running miles ahead of anybody's ability to sum it up. The young are in one another's arms. They are in one another's books. The A & R Modern Poets series has done well to include some of the younger talents, among whom it is not absurd to count David Malouf, who is in his early fifties but so obviously only half-embarked on his prodigious career that he ranks as a beginner. In Malouf's poems the whole complex theme of Australia's position in regard to the world which supplied its modern population is, if not wrapped up, at least raised up and illuminated.

> The nineteen tongues of Europe
> migrate to fill a silence, we're digging in for the long wait.

Malouf, like Josef Brodsky, is a culture-vulture with the range and cruising altitude of a condor. They are both men with a mission. Brodsky's mission is to represent his country in exile. Malouf's is to help build a new country by pouring his background into its foundations. These are very different tasks, but theirs are not very different talents. They share the seductive gift of being able to objectify, in a passing phrase, that feeling which Osip Mandelstam called nostalgia for a world culture.

Nostalgia it must remain. To the extent that a world culture can actually exist, it can only be banal. It wears a J. R. Ewing T-shirt. As nations acquire individuality, they must become less knowable. To grow up is to grow apart. Adults are strangers to one another. The best that Australia can do, with regard to Britain and all the other European nations still less lucky – the best that it can do even with regard to America, which sounds so close but is really further away than anywhere – is to welcome the necessary disjunction, to construct strong and airy bridges, to make light of it.

The Australian poets of today may legitimately complain about the world and their country's place in it, but they can no longer complain about their place in their country. The days when they were not taken seriously are over. Now, in a land gone mad about art, they are taken so seriously that they should beware. Australia is in danger of producing an artistic class. In the nineteenth century, the ideal of an Australian art-form was one which did not leave the people out. The poets wrote ballads not because they couldn't do otherwise, but because they sought democracy. With high culture in Australia increasingly well taken care of, not to say pampered, nevertheless the old challenge still nags. This year, as in any other year, the publishing event in Australian poetry is the latest, umpteenth edition of C. J. Dennis's *Sentimental Bloke*. When an Australian poet writes something as genuinely popular as *that* again, the critics at home will at last have something to write abroad about.

The Times Literary Supplement
27 November–3 December, 1987

Your Space or Mine?

(*The Road to Botany Bay* by Paul Carter, Faber, 1987)
(*The Oxford History of Australia. Vol. IV: 1901–1942* by Stuart
Macintyre, Oxford, 1987)
(*The Archibald Paradox: A Strange Case of Authorship* by
Sylvia Lawson, Penguin Australia, 1987)
(*The Lucky Country Revisited* by Donald Horne, Dent, 1987)

IN ITS short history, Australia has weathered several
storms. By world standards they were minor, but at
home they loomed large. The First World War was a rude
awakening; the Great Depression hit harder and lasted
longer than anywhere else in the developed world; and the
Second World War could have been the end of everything.
Australia survived all these crises and given its usual luck
should also survive the Bicentenary, although it could be
touch and go.

Crocodile Dundee made Australia flavour of the month.
For the Bicentenary, emulsifiers and preservatives have
been added so as to make the flavour of the month last a
whole year. Inevitably, the result is hard to swallow. A
country is not a commodity. To treat it like one, you must
submit yourself to market forces, and to the eventual discovery of just how forceful those forces can be. When publicity
swamps reality, it leaves tacky deposits as it withdraws.
1989 is going to be tough. Australia, however, will still be
there, perhaps even with its inborn scepticism reinforced,
more worldly-wise for having just been overwhelmed.

Australian prose is at its most characteristic when
ready-salted. On the whole, Australian journalists have
written better history, or at any rate better-written history,
than the historians, among whom Geoffrey Blainey –
whose *The Tyranny of Distance* must count as the single most

original historical work about Australia – is exceptional in possessing an individual style. Manning Clark, doyen of Australian historians by virtue of his five-volume *History of Australia*, in scholarship towers over all his predecessors but writes no better. Here, drawn from *A Short History of Australia*, the indispensable one-volume condensation of his *magnum opus*, is a by no means atypical sentence: 'The choir sang a Te Deum, which because of the terrible heat wafted fitfully around the arena; the flag of the new commonwealth was hoisted, and the artillery thundered and cheer after cheer ran around the great arena.'

You don't need the stylistic scrupulousness of Turgenev to see that the use of the word 'great', if it was intended to offset the repetition of the word 'arena', had the opposite effect. But it is more likely that the perpetrator simply never noticed. Let alone re-write, he doesn't even re-read. He leaves the reader to do that. Try this: 'In the mean time the Australian and New Zealand expeditionary force trained for war at their camp near Cairo, and relaxed and pursued pleasure in the cafés and low dives of Cairo . . .'

Is this, the reader hopefully asks, a rhetorical device, an obeisance towards the cool symmetry of the Gibbonian period? The reader soon gives up asking. Tolstoy didn't mind repeating a word, but knew he was doing it. Manning Clark doesn't know. But he does know his own mind. He might use the word 'bourgeois' twenty times per chapter but he knows what he means by it. He means the capitalist society which Australia has always persisted in remaining, even when presented with the opportunity to become something else. You can object to Clark's view – I do, and what's more important my mother, who elects the government, does too – but you can tell exactly what he means at all times. He means business.

What Paul Carter means in *The Road to Botany Bay* is either something more profound or else nothing at all. Unless I am a Dutchman, he means the latter, but I should say, before hacking into it, that his book comes laden with wreaths of praise, a true triumphal car of the bicentennial celebrations. 'The writing has a lyrical passion in argument that I found irresistible,' says no less a judge than David Malouf. 'I couldn't put it down.' Malouf being no fool, I am reluctant to suggest that the reason he couldn't put the book down was that it is so full of hot air it kept springing back up again. Reluctant, but compelled.

Lyrically passionate writing should always be resisted, especially by the writer. A real idea slows you down, by demanding that you make yourself as plain as possible. A big idea – the nice name for a hazy notion – speeds you up. You try to find out what you mean by examining the words in which you say it, by mixing one abstract concept into another as if two kinds of sand could make cement, by suddenly *switching to italics* as if a breakthrough into clear country had been achieved by hard sweat. Mr Carter's big idea is that most of the history written about Australia up to now has been imperial history. He has invented a better version, called spatial history. The word 'spatial' recurs in Mr Carter's prose the way 'bourgeois' does in Manning Clark's, with the difference that whereas Professor Clark's favourite word is gravid with dull significance, Mr Carter's is as brightly hollow as a Christmas bauble. Here he is, at the start of his book, announcing that Manning Clark's kind of history,

> which reduces space to a stage, that pays attention to events unfolding in time alone, might be called imperial history. The governor erects a tent here rather than there, the soldier blazes a trail in that direction rather than this: but, rather than focus on the *intentional* world of historical individuals, the world of active, spatial choices, empirical history of this kind has as its focus facts which, in a sense, come after the event. The primary object is not to understand or to interpret: it is to legitimate. This is why this history is associated with imperialism . . .

Mr Carter well knows that to call Manning Clark an imperialist historian is like saying that Bertolt Brecht had a crush on the Duchess of Windsor. But big ideas go beyond what the mind that hatches them knows: they fly into the realm where thought is pure. Mr Carter has got himself convinced that even though a historian might be a radical, the history the historian writes is imperial, because it not only sees the past in terms of what happened next, it sees a *space* in terms of how it turned into a *place*. To combat imperial history, and turn the places back into spaces, spatial history will be required. 'Such spatial history – history that discovers and explores the lacuna left by imperial history – begins and ends in language.' The reader can't say that he hasn't been warned.

Imperial history, 'the selective blandnesses of cultural discourse', has apparently been going on since the Enlightenment. If it has, then Mr Carter is in the uncomfortable position of holding himself superior to some pretty formidable minds. He doesn't say how it came about that his own viewpoint should be so uniquely privileged, although, judging from his vocabulary, structuralism, semiotics and similar fashions must have had a good deal to do with it. The phrase 'ways of seeing' crops up, reminding us of John Berger and his allegedly penetrating double squint. The authorial assumption which remains unquestioned at the end of the book – after 350 pages in which the word 'spatial' appears rarely fewer than three times per paragraph and sometimes twice in the same sentence – is that an alternative to imperial history, namely spatial history, is not just possible but mandatory, in order to right age-old wrongs. Spatial history would, for example, have the virtue of being fair to the Aborigines.

> A spatial history of this kind would stand in a metaphorical relationship to the history the Aborigines tell themselves. It would be a comparable reflection on different historical content. And, naturally, since the medium of white history is writing, it would not simply be a book about the language of recollection. If it were to avoid the kind of passive associationism Husserl refers to, it would have to enact the language of recollection. Such a history, giving back to metaphor

its ontological role and recovering its historical space,
would inevitably and properly be a poetic history.

I wouldn't bet on it, unless the historian could write
plain English in the first place. A few weeks ago in Sydney
I had a drink with an Aboriginal actor called Ernie Dingo,
who talked more poetry in five minutes than Mr Carter
looks like achieving in the rest of his life, unless Husserl
is forcibly withheld from him. The sad thing is that in
real life Mr Carter is a literary journalist of some repute.
As Robert Haupt's successor to the editorship of the *Age
Monthly Review*, he inhabits a milieu, or space, in which the
standards of plain speaking were set by the redoubtable
Michael Davie, who really should get back there and sort
out his errant protégés as soon as possible.

Good journalists should not waste time producing bad
PhD theses. In the academic context there is some reason
for the success of pseudo-scientific guff: emptying the
humanities of their true significance is a way of attaining
tenure without talent. But a journalist who tries to join in
is just talking his way into the madhouse. There are signs
that Mr Carter might know this, deep down. It must have
been some vestigial attack of sanity that led him, on page
294, to attempt a definition of the word 'bullshit'. 'Bullshit
is the result of chewing the cud, the repetitive detritus of
trying too hard to conjure oneself from the ground.' *Ipse
dixit.*

More briefly, bullshit is empty depth. Mr Carter feels
obliged to deploy his chic vocabulary not because his big
idea is new but because it is a truism. Gibbon was well
aware that Rome was a space before it was a place, and
got the idea for writing his history when he saw the space
re-emerging through the place's ruins. Those who do not
think originally enough to be interesting when they write
plainly will always be tempted to seek refuge in obscurant-
ism, but a journalist, if he can do nothing else, should resist
that temptation. After *The Road to Botany Bay*, Australian
history might as well be left to the historians.

Stuart Macintyre, author of the fourth volume of the

Oxford History of Australia, covers the years 1901–1942 in good plain style, with words like 'bourgeois' kept well in check and words like 'spatial' nowhere to be seen. Aiming to get at the truth, which is always more complicated than any use that can be made of it, he delivers the sort of factual account which ideologists of either wing find awkward. He mentions that the British lost three times as many soldiers killed at Gallipoli as the Australians did – a fact left out of the celebrated Australian film *Gallipoli*, in which the British appear only as cynical manipulators of Australian cannon-fodder. He mentions, on the other hand, that the Australians came out of the Dardanelles with a deep, well-founded disbelief in British military competence.

Even in his grave, Robert Gordon Menzies is regularly vilified as the Australian prime minister who would do anything for the British, including offering up his young compatriots as a blood sacrifice. Dr Macintyre is able to show that Menzies, though his bump of reverence was undoubtedly overdeveloped, was properly suspicious of Churchill and patriotically concerned that Australian troops should not be frittered away far from home. The book ends at what is seen, surely correctly, as a decisive historical moment. Succeeding Menzies as prime minister, John Curtin proclaimed the alliance with the United States to be the one that mattered militarily. At the battle of the Coral Sea the Americans stopped the Japanese from getting under New Guinea. In the Owen Stanley ranges the Australians stopped the Japanese from getting across it. The two events were interdependent.

The Australians can be proud of how their soldiers fought, but without the American effort the game would have been up. British protection was a myth that evaporated with the fall of Singapore. Dr Macintyre faithfully repeats the hoary story about Singapore's big guns facing the wrong way. Actually they could traverse through 360 degrees. The trouble with them was their ammunition, which was armour-piercing for use against ships, and which therefore, when fired against targets on the soft ground of the mainland, went off plop among the mangroves. We had plenty of other guns, but their ammunition was rationed, by strict order of General Percival. See, as Dr Macintyre evidently hasn't seen, Timothy Hall's journalistic but competent account *The Fall of Singapore, 1942.*

British military ineptitude in Malaya was almost total. Dr Macintyre is within his rights to say that the Australian general staff were not much better, but he should have mentioned that we had some good officers up near the fighting. Some of the greener troops behaved badly on the Singapore docks, but on the mainland – at Parit Sulong bridge, for example – our soldiers slowed the Japanese down to a degree that could have been exploited if there had been any kind of strategic grasp at command level. All of that, however, belonged to General Yamashita, whose Imperial Guards, had they ever got ashore in Australia, might well have turned it back from a place into a space, as a preparation for its being transformed into another kind of place altogether.

The last chapter of Dr Macintyre's book is disproportionate through being only the same length as all the others. In actuality, two years of war weighed the same as twenty years of peace, because the war changed everything. In this way, history really *is* like space: tumultuous events set apart from each other, and connected by gravity. Responding to its rhythm is not easy. A metronomic beat won't do. *Rubato* is required.

Some of the best Australian history is cultural history, not just because better written, but because the culturati, eternally anxious to place themselves in a context, try hard to evoke it. Sylvia Lawson, a descendant of Henry Lawson, was a pioneer – *the* pioneer – Australian woman literary journalist in the Fifties. In the editorial office of Tom Fitzgerald's *Nation* magazine in George Street, Sydney, she would elegantly sip the wine provided while the rest of us tried to mention a book she hadn't read. It wasn't easy, and writing as well as she did was no less of a challenge. Thirty years on, her new book *The Archibald Paradox* is disturbingly flecked throughout with words like 'text' and 'discourse', but on close examination this proves to be more of a light peppering than a full attack of the plague. Underneath, she is still a tough-minded writer, and this book springs from a real, as opposed to a big, idea.

The idea is that the famous Sydney weekly magazine the *Bulletin* was, in the twenty or so years leading up to Federation, even more interesting in the totality of its content – letters column included – than it was for its individual literary contributions. The Archibald of the title was the magazine's editor, Jules François Archibald, the embodiment of a paradox which Ms Lawson usefully defines: 'To know enough of the metropolitan world, colonials must, in limited ways at least, move and think internationally; to resist it strongly enough for the colony to cease to be colonial and become its own place, they must become nationalists.'

Archibald lived out this paradox through the pages of his magazine. Within the accepted racist limits ('Australia for the White Man,' screamed the masthead at one stage, 'and China for the Chows') the *Bulletin* was a true community of voices. Every shade of white was represented. Archibald's appointee as literary editor, Alfred George Stephens, was an erudite critic who brought a full range of Europeanised refinement to the task of assessing raw native talent. The whole of the country came alive in the *Bulletin* and the whole of its history in that period comes alive in Ms Lawson's book. So solid an achievement didn't need to make the slightest gesture towards academic respectability.

When Donald Horne took over the *Bulletin* in 1961, he killed off the slogan 'Australia for the White Man'. Self-assurance was, and remains, his strong suit. Horne's writing about Australian cultural history and current affairs is a cut above journalism in a country whose journalism, at its best, has always had the virtue of being willing to get above itself. *The Lucky Country Revisited* expands on and continues the story told in his *The Lucky Country*, a book which remains essential but can only gain through being supplemented by this new volume, which includes many photographs with appropriately extended captions, along with much judicious hindsight tartly expressed.

All over again it becomes clear that Australian cultural history is the best way into Australian history, and that the best way into Australian cultural history, in modern times at any rate, is through Horne's books. His autobiographical volumes, in particular, should be high on the reading list of any foreign observer who wants to take the measure of what has been going on in Australia since World War Two. Horne's second volume of autobiography, *Confessions of a New Boy*, was on my draft list of Books of the Year for the *Observer* the year before last, but I was made to remove it because it had not been published here. Peeved at the time, I subsequently arrived at the conclusion that a good Australian book no longer needs to be legitimised by being published all over again in the UK. Horne has resolved the Archibald paradox as well as anyone can. Bringing a world view to bear on his native land, he hammers its provincialism, but always as a patriot. His kind of sceptical intelligence is exactly what the Australians fancy themselves to possess as a national characteristic, and exactly what makes them uncomfortable when they hear it propound a connected argument.

In the field of arts, letters and the *petit bonheur*, Horne is well pleased by the giant strides Australia has made away from its erstwhile diffidence and wowserism, but the vaunted energy and imagination of its entrepreneurs leave him unimpressed. In *The Lucky Country Revisited* his perennial dim view of the Australian managerial élite is brought up to date and reinforced. Horne's argument will ring a bell for those of us who have always wondered why someone who buys a brewery with money made out of lousy newspapers is called a financial genius. But Horne is not pandering to the highbrow who despises industry. Horne thinks that if the entrepreneurs are living in a dream, the intellectuals are doing too little to dispel it.

I wish Horne wasn't right about this, because Australia would be a blissful place in which to inhabit an ivory tower – you could see the beach for miles. Dreaming, however, might do for us in the end, and needs more discouragement than it is getting now. The cure is realism.

Australian historians suffer from having too little history to work on. But there is plenty more coming up, and although we can't be sure what will happen, we can be sure we won't like it, unless those who take on the task of putting the past in perspective are thoughtful and disciplined enough to give us a reasonably clear account of how we got this far.

London Review of Books
18 February, 1988

Fanfare for a Big Yin

(A note for the theatre programme of Billy Connolly's
one-man show at the Hammersmith Odeon, 1991)

BILLY CONNOLLY is a man loved even by those who
hate him. A press photographer who was once punched
in the mouth by Billy Connolly has been heard to say: 'I
lumpf hmmff lime own brummumf.' Billy Connolly is the
tough product of an even tougher environment. He was
raised in the toughest area of Glasgow, a town so tough
that a lot of people refuse to go there. Almost the entire
population of the Soviet Union, for example, have never
even mentioned the place except when mispronouncing
the word *glasnost* during heated arguments around the
samovar. The baby Billy was handed the unopened bottle
of milk and told to get on with it. He has been getting on
with it ever since. He is, above all, a *dynamic* comedian. He
moves with the balletic grace of a ballet dancer in . . . a
ballet. His extension is terrifying in its completeness. He
puts out one foot, slaps it on the floor in front of him,
and looks at it. With his exquisite hands pinching the
air at each side of the respective shoulder, he continues
to look at that foot. Is there another one like it? Why yes,
there is! Triumphantly he produces it and slaps it on the
floor beside the other. His cry of triumph is drowned by a
squeal of pain as he falls over backwards. But within weeks
he is back on his feet, ready, before the gale of laughter has
subsided, to continue with his non-stop stream of jest and
antidote.

To be serious for a moment, though I court solem-
nity, let me say that Billy Connolly has the great
secret of uttering the unutterable. He is outrageous, but
he is never foul-mouthed. What he says could be said by

the Archbishop of Canterbury to any audience of Mongol
storm-troopers on a three-day pass. Finally, he is funny. He
knows who you are. He knows what you do when you are
alone. But then so, you might object, did Sigmund Freud.
What a Viennese psychoanalytic genius couldn't do in a
lifetime, however, Billy Connolly can do in the twinkling
of an eye. He can put you in touch with your secret self.
You fall on each other's necks, crying: 'Fancy meeting *you*
here!'

Punching a sudden hole through the wall of our
amour propre and filling the aperture with his hirsute,
wildly staring visage, Billy Connolly reminds us that within the tungsten carapace of our dignity quivers a secret
nosepicker. We forgive him. We forgive him everything
except his talent. Those of us who have to sweat over
our secretaries all day waiting for that rare moment when
an idea comes unbidden can have only one reaction when
we hear this supernaturally gifted man in the ecstatic
throes of making the stuff up even faster than he can
spit it out. In tones of hushed awe we say '**@£&1/8%
him.' Too much talent, too much life – and on top of that
he is generous, gregarious, gentle and compassionate. No
wonder Billy Connolly is a man hated even by those who
love him.

Sarah Raphael

(An introductory essay to the catalogue for her exhibition at Agnew's Gallery in Bond Street, February 1992)

S OMETHING WONDERFUL happened to her in an art gallery, and something terrible in the park. One's first impression of Sarah Raphael's painting can be no less complex than that. It would be nice simply to be bowled over. She doesn't allow it. If you saw just the early oils; or just the drawings; or just the portraits – but no, the turbulence would already be stirring in the viewer's psyche. The individual portraits are among the most desirable being done in Britain today. Anyone who can catch her eye, or afford the tab, or whatever it is that needs doing so that she will get interested in making you look interesting, would like to sit for Sarah Raphael. I sat, and I'm still wondering about the result. I am bound to say that I rather like the immediate message of macho power, reinforced by those Iron John forearms. If only I didn't look so very isolated and inward-turned, as if self-sufficiency had been bought at the cost of losing contact with the world. That can't be right, but what if it is? What if she knows better than I do?

My portrait isn't in the present exhibition, and that suits me. It's not quite that I feel about my portrait by Sarah Raphael the way Winston Churchill felt about his by Graham Sutherland, but if it was being displayed in public I'd like to be standing beside it to *explain*: to bob and smile and try to get a bit of charm going. Sarah Raphael is either very keen on taking the charm out, or else she just sees things as if it wasn't there. Even the most seductive of the portraits would hint that the latter is true, and when you see her major paintings, especially the later ones in acrylic, there can be no doubt about it; a determined attempt is being mounted to deprettify the world – and not just the physical world but the psychological one as well.

In one so young the aim would be insupportable if it were not backed up by such accomplishment. We know she is an artist, because her bad dreams are contained – sometimes barely contained, but always contained – in beautiful painting. We know she is serious because she is so staunchly resistant to the mere notion of painting something lovely for its own sake – even though, especially though, she could. She has the basic belief and the inescapable curse of any serious artist in any field: for her, all technical problems are moral ones and vice versa. There are great artists who have come slowly to that realisation. Sarah Raphael apparently arrived at it during adolescence. Precocious technicians we can cope with: we call them prodigies. Artists who are precocious in their moral maturity are more of a problem. The Rimbaud who got shot by Verlaine is a less troublesome customer than the one who wrote *Bateau ivre*.

To invite discussion on the level of great names might not be a blessing for Sarah Raphael, especially in Britain, where any failure to disclaim big-league ambitions is counted as arrogance, as if to seek exemption from comparative assessment were somehow more modest. But Sarah Raphael is stuck by nature with the status of one who can't absorb an influence without seeming to compete with it on equal terms. The parodist apes his model from a flea's eye view. The artist takes over a whole soul. Poussin and Rembrandt took over galleries of souls: you can see complete traditions being mopped up. It was scarily apparent after only the first few big oils of Sarah Raphael's early phase that she was doing the same sort of thing.

Those were the paintings of hers that are still easiest to like. She was using a wide range of colour and the canvas was full of individual characters even if they mostly stared past each other with minimum eye contact. But admirable as well as likeable, and remarkable as well as admirable, was the rate and the intensity with which

74

she soaked up and summed up influence, as if the whole western tradition of painting was queueing up to get into her mind and she had her work cut out assigning places so that the different painters would have something to say to one another instead of crowding around in awkward groups or just sitting in each other's laps. Under colonnades out of Crivelli stalked figures out of Piero della Francesca and Paolo Uccello's Green Cloister frescoes in Santa Maria Novella, forming tableaux that would have had the unmanning elegance of Max Liebermann if they had not been as monumental as Max Beckmann. She had rediscovered, out of a radically revamped past, the quattrocento version of the *Neue Sachlichkeit*. It was weird, wild and excessively gifted and your first instinct was to take it away from her. A girl her age needed an artistic capability about the size and power of a Citroen 2CV, and she had turned up at the wheel of a Ferrari.

Since then we have got used to it. Time tatters the prodigy tag, and besides, our fears for her were soon revealed to be fears for ourselves. She could easily have gone wrong if she had been us. Not only high society, but show business or just any prosperous demographic group with a collective ego to embalm, would have been glad to deflect her from her course. Personally personable, she could have engaged full-time in manufacturing her own publicity, with no danger, in her case, of the supply ever outstripping the demand. (When I wrote a brief introductory piece about her for *Interview*, the magazine sent a madly fashionable photographer who required her to dress in a unicorn's head and nothing else. The results were electrifying. Tamara de Lempicka never managed to set up a photo session like that in her whole life.) The unsettling truth was that there was never any chance that our delighted dread of yet another crashed young talent would come about. Her ambitions went beyond success and deep into the more serious business of getting something inside her that needed saying out into the open where it would require seeing: require and command.

Her command of her resources gave her command

75

of our attention. The oils already had authority, saying 'I am younger than you but I see all this.' On one of my walls – my tallest wall – is a very large Sarah Raphael oil with a small mirror in the middle of it in which the painter is reflected. It is an honest portrait of her and therefore very striking, because so is she. In the bottom left-hand corner of the canvas, bulking grotesquely beside the table under the mirror, is a chunky dwarf out of Velázquez. The painting wants me to realise that beauty and ugliness are both accidents. Most of us are as slow to accept such facts as we can get away with. When Sarah Raphael switched to acrylic she increased her authoritative capacity to put our own fears in front of us in forms we would have to face because they were too compactly composed to ignore. She began to restrict her range of colour into a narrow, aching band of grey, deep green and a strange sky blue that isn't precisely dark but somehow never gets light enough to relax by. Often the scene is a park, and anyone on his own is threatened by any group no matter how small or distant.

In the oils the potential for atrocity was at least lit up and relatively festive, like the matinée pogrom in Cossa's Schifanoia fresco. In the acrylics the overcast has penetrated to the bone. There are brilliant colours, especially in the clothes of children, but they are not allowed to radiate. Once there was a British musical film, *Elstree Calling*, in which each of the three primary colours was added to a separate black-and-white image and then the three images were added together. The result was in colour but weighed like uranium. For her own purposes, Sarah Raphael wants us to feel that from the memory of universal anguish there is no recourse in the spectrum.

The question remains of what those purposes are. Primarily, surely, they must be to let her inner demons run. Born into a personal history for which the most immediately appropriate symbol would surely be the Holocaust, she derives her most upsetting imagery from the Crucifixion. But she has distanced the event only to deal more directly with the emotion. The emotion is fear: our fear, modern fear, twentieth-century fear. In previous times people were afraid of casual violence. But we are afraid of the casual violence that ought not to be there – the policemen who persecute, the doctor who tortures, the apparatus of the state that goes to war with the citizen. Above all we are afraid that our hard-won understanding of the human mind has failed to tame the primitive, and that the beast can drive a car and knows when our daughter gets out of school.

Most of my favourite paintings were painted by Australian impressionists on the lids of cigar boxes. The only challenge they offer is not to be charmed to death. As safely conservative in my basic taste as a Japanese industrialist chasing any Monet left on the market, I would prefer on the whole that artists did not explore, and were content to entertain. Hankering incorrigibly for Picasso's Blue and Rose, I still can't look at his damsels on the beach without crying subvocally 'Don't do it to us, Pablo!' But I would be a lesser man spiritually if I got my preference. To look at the recent haunted landscapes of Sarah Raphael, lit by storm clouds and swept by a slow, chill wind of truth, is to pine for those relatively untroubled early oils in which the merchants of the ghetto found at least a fleeting home under the portico, and girls who knew Balthus were framed by Bramante. But that is part of her point. She wants to get beyond what comforts and into what liberates. We trust her to unmask our imagination because we know the magnitude of the talents with which she might flatter it if she wished.

Speaking for myself, I would like to see a new synthesis, in which the psychoanalytic investigations of her maturity might be lit up with the carnival colours of her apprenticeship. But if she catered to nostalgia she wouldn't be what she is, and meanwhile the portraits are there to work the instant enchantment. They do more than that, but they always do that in the first moment, private and alone yet invading the eye with the unnerving confidence of a stranger who expects to be recognised. The portraits are her guarantee of discipline, a constant life class. They are also the playground for her technique, in the same way that Mozart returned always to the piano concerto as his test-bed for the new engine, his wind-tunnel for the new wing. It would take a structuralist critic of outstanding ruthlessness to separate her portraiture from personality, but if it could be done there would still be a technical story to be considered. I am not qualified to consider it, but would guess that it had something to do with making acrylic yield all the nuances of oil without the smarm. Acrylic to this painter is what rhyme is to a proper poet: the obstacle which furnishes the departure point for inspiration.

And a proper painter she is. The most effective subversives are well brought up. Raised in a house where the arts are talked about as if they were a part of life – it remains amazing how rare that is in England, especially among the educated – she was trained in her craft before she practised it as an art, and so is able to draw and paint ahead of her ideas. She is one of the young figurative painters whose success enables us to feel relieved that the meaningful was never entirely swept away by the meaningless, only mostly. The market for the temporarily immortalised gesture still has some buoyancy in it: according to a recent Christie's catalogue, you can get a Lucian Freud portrait for only £40,000 but a Cy Twombly assemblage of several different-coloured squiggles will still set you back a healthy two and a half million dollars. The market, however, is a moron, and art – real art – has a mind of its own. Finally it is in the keeping of those with talent, and the truly talented, whatever the circumstances, will be damned before they do less than what is in them. Sarah Raphael has so much to say that she has not yet quite become used to the idea of getting it said in one epic at a time. To watch her find her way is a privilege.

We Shall Be Re-released

(Sleeve notes for Pete Atkin's retrospective album
Touch Has A Memory, 1991)

A IMING AT a minority in a market that catered exclusively
to majorities, we were doomed, Pete Atkin and I, but
it took us almost ten years to admit it, and in that time we
wrote these songs. Even at this distance, I wouldn't claim
to be objective about their quality. Subjectively, though, I
have always thought of them as the most intense creative
endeavour I was ever mixed up in. Writing the words for
Pete's music, I had that feeling every writer gets when he
is on to a good thing. I suppose carpenters get it too, when
they are planing with the grain. It was the way to go. Since
those days I have written books that got more attention
than my lyrics, and TV shows that made more money,
but nothing else has generated quite that euphoria.

Unfortunately you can't eat euphoria. Like good
reviews, which we also had plenty of, it nourishes only
the soul. In those days the magic adjective was 'commercial'. If a song wasn't commercial, it aroused grave doubts
among music business executives. These latter were usually
even younger than we were and always incomparably more
hip. Pete and I had flared trousers too, but the music business executives had hair styles which indicated many hours
of rapt communication with the blow-drier. Through long
lunches they explained to us, in widely spaced words of one
syllable, why things would be so much simpler if we could
take a more commercial approach. (The word 'commercial',
of course, has three syllables, but not the way they said it.)

They were right. Things *would* have been simpler.
But we had stuck ourselves with the most uncommer-
cial approach possible. A fiercely loyal, highly intelligent

79

audience who understood every nuance and subtlety – and from whom we both still get letters – would purchase every album Pete put out. Alas, commercial success depended on roping in a tangible percentage of all those other people as well.

Perhaps we were behind the times. I like to think that we were ahead of them, and that the era our work really fits into is beginning now. What we were up to – as far as I can tell as a participant – was a sort of post-modern synthesis. At that time you couldn't be post-modern, because everyone was modern. People were young in those days, and very sure of themselves. In the Sixties and early Seventies, the past began in the Fifties. If you said you respected Tin Pan Alley, you were thought of as a throw-back. Today, and not just because nostalgia has become an industry, there is a greater willingness to rummage in an older dressing-up box than the one that holds the loon pants, the tie-dyed T-shirts, the head-bands and the beads.

When Pete and I began to write together for the Cambridge Footlights, popular music was already providing some brilliantly witty work. On the whole, then as now, the popular song was dedicated either to saying something mindless memorably or else to embalming an alleged profundity in semi-literate bathos. But there were exceptions, and how they shone. Pete used to buy the Mamas and Papas albums as they came out, and I still own everything by Randy Newman. John Sebastian's songs for the Lovin' Spoonful were among our touchstones. The Holland-Dozier-Holland hits for Motown showed how strokes of seeming simplicity could build into a perfectly satisfactory pattern. We kept in touch with all these developments. I wrote long, ponderous articles for *Cream* about Joni Mitchell and Bob Dylan. But what really drove us was the achievement of the previous generation and the generation before that. Before the singer-songwriters, there were the song-writers.

Before I met Pete, I already knew my way around the lyrics of Cole Porter, Lorenz Hart, Ira Gershwin and Johnny Mercer. Pete knew all that and more. On the Footlights stage, at a quarter to three, with no-one in the place except him and me, he would take me through those pages of the Mercer-Arlen song-book that had been stuck together with coffee-stains and bitter tears. There was a song by Tad Dameron I had never heard before. From the very first, we wanted to write songs that got all those possibilities in.

My own particular urge was to use all the words in a song that I might possibly use in any other medium, including the scholarly footnote. This occasionally led to excess. Later on we were sometimes accused of wordiness, and sometimes it was true. Usually, though, we were pushing things to the limit in full confidence that the limit lay a good way beyond where it was supposed to be. After all, our heroes of days gone by had done the same.

For some of the songs I wrote the words first and then Pete wrote the music. For others Pete wrote the music first and then I wrote the words. In the majority of cases, as I remember, we worked together at the same time, repeatedly meeting and mutually modifying. 'As I remember', however, is a phrase that by now belongs in a song itself, because the truth is that I would be hard pressed to describe exactly how we did it. We wrote songs in Footlights and in the kitchen of the communal flat we inhabited at the Edinburgh Festival; and then in our walk-up flat in Swiss Cottage, and later on in Islington; and between studio dates for our London Weekend song-show series *The Party's Moving On*, which has no doubt all been wiped: and even at Morgan sound studios, where Pete recorded his albums on budgets that wouldn't have paid for the sandwiches the members of Yes ate while they clumped around on built-up clogs, we would be writing new songs in the bar.

Year after year, every song we wrote resolutely declined to be commercial. Val Doonican's cover version of *The Flowers and the Wine* made more money than all our other efforts put together. Eventually we had to stop. But our songs, it turned out, had what we had always hoped for them to have – a life of their own. Those marvellous people who bought them hung on to them, and now here they are again.

He That Played the Fool

(*The Life of Kenneth Tynan* by Kathleen Tynan,
Weidenfeld, 1987)

K ENNETH TYNAN had it to burn, so he burned it.
The greatest critical talent since Shaw threw it all
away. That, at any rate, is the generally accepted idea,
which Kathleen Tynan's biography, well written though
it is, and even though it tries to do the opposite, can only
reinforce. It's the wrong idea, but it can't lose. To explain
the man makes him less dazzling. It helps cut his intensity
down to size. Put out the light, and then put out the light.

Some such process of diminishment would have
been inevitable, even if its subject had not appeared
so enthusiastically to co-operate. Tynan wrote too well to
be easily put up with by other cultural journalists. Even
when they praised him they were looking for a weakness.
In his early days, a weakness was hard to find. In his very
early days he was even better than that.

For Tynan at Oxford and just after, the term genius
seems not out of place. Certainly there is no precocity
to match his in the whole of English prose. You would have
to go to the novels of Radiguet or the plays of Büchner to
find a parallel. His first collection, *He That Plays the King*
– everything in it composed before he even got to Fleet
Street – is a classic book which, were it to be republished
now in its slim entirety, might give the new generation of
journalists in the cultural field a salutary fright.

In places, Tynan's astonishing first book is as
precious as 'The Unquiet Grave'. There are passages
that out-posture Palinurus. But you can put that down
to his age (twenty-three), exacerbated by *the* age – that
period of post-war austerity which produced, as a reaction, *Brideshead Revisited* and the verse plays of Christopher

Fry. What makes the collection timeless is Tynan's wit, and there is seldom anything precious about that. Tynan could make his prose speak right out of the page: he had the essential button-holing gift of the star critic.

Tynan's ostensible business, in those early days, was with heroic acting, of which, indeed, he was a peerless anatomist. But while in search of what he admired he had to see much which he did not, and about that he had the valuable gift of being amusing. 'Joyce Redman tried unwisely to make novel use of her buxom build and strident voice by playing a strong, commanding Cordelia. Her best time came after she was dead.' This is tough but not cruel, because it leaves the actress the possibility of being good in other parts, or in the same part played a different way. About Eileen Herlie, playing Medea at the 1948 Edinburgh Festival, he *was* cruel. 'I admit that in repose she is gracious: but she lunges rather than moves, and she has common hands.' Tynan was lucky to wake up next morning without finding his victim's hands fastened around his neck. In pursuit of his passion, he had forgotten her feelings, or anyway, forgotten that they mattered.

His passion was for theatre. This is what so sharply distinguishes Tynan's wit from that of previous critics whose writings are generally attributed with that quality, but who were in fact not theatre critics at all. Dorothy Parker, for example, funny though she could be, knew nothing about the theatre and had no judgment of it. She was using it as an opportunity to make wisecracks. Tynan's imperative was the very opposite. He was enslaved to the theatre. You can tell by the way he praised the great moments of his heroic actors: Olivier, Gielgud, Richardson, Wolfit, Guinness. If they tended to remember how he dispraised their weak moments, even the most bitter among them were obliged to concede that he was merciless only out of a sense of duty to high ideals. Tynan had theatre instead of religion.

He also had it instead of politics. Later on, when he got interested in politics, he treated them as theatre, which is perhaps the clue to his later diffuseness. Orson

Welles, in the preface which he contributed to *He That Plays the King* (the young author, whom Welles did not know, pressed the manuscript on him unsolicited, and Welles, in one of history's few recorded cases of genius recognising genius first off, coughed up a free plug), spotted a tendency which Tynan spent the rest of his life trying to deal with – 'a confusion between high glamour and tragic truth.'

The words are Welles's but the trouble was Tynan's. In everything from how he dressed to what he worshipped, Tynan behaved as if purity could be attained just by screwing theatricality up to a high enough pitch. Somewhere in that assumption was an irreconcilable contradiction. He was under no obligation to reconcile it. Merely to have identified it and discussed it would have kept him going for a fruitful lifetime into a wise old age. But the drama within himself was the only one he could not review.

Kathleen Tynan, made well aware of this fact by the sad end it led to, tries hard and honourably to find reasons. It is not the first honour she has done him. She honoured him by putting up with him when he proved, like so many writers, to be no better fitted for married life than for self-propelled flight; and now she has honoured him by writing a book brave enough to take him seriously at the level where he came, in later years, to think himself most serious – as an assault pioneer of the sexual-political revolution. There can be no doubt that he would have thanked her for taking such a dare, so it would be niggardly of the onlooker not to thank her as well. One wonders, though, whether she has really uncovered much by revealing all. It is possible to lay a false trail with discarded veils.

Let no-one doubt her bravery. Her husband, on this evidence, was a psychological disaster-area. His own explanation for his kinky sexuality was an identity crisis dating from his illegitimate childhood. On the other hand, he came to regard his kinky sexuality as a form of expression, with a right to be heard. He started off with the worthy aim of wanting to abolish the Lord Chamberlain and ended up with the less endearing determination to dress up as Louise Brooks. It was the usual story of a man being caught up with by the era he helped instigate, and making a guy of himself by trying to outrun it. But it meant harrowing times for his biographer, who can be forgiven for painting a picture of that sensitive face, skull-like from the beginning, being eaten up by the anguish within.

Such turmoil would explain anyone's decline. Perhaps, however, it explains itself. Tynan's penchant for transsexual dressing and the milder forms of flagellation did not cramp his prose style in the first place, so why should it have done so later on? When the marvellous boy hit Fleet Street, he went as far as his gift could take him – all the way to immortality.

Readers of the *Observer* could turn to his column and find sentences good enough to leave their breakfast cold. 'His tragedy,' Tynan said of Uncle Vanya, 'is that he is capable only of comedy.' Shaw himself is no comparison: you have to go back to Coleridge to find so much character analysis in such a short space.

Tynan became a force for good in the theatre. He helped raise its intelligence by the way he criticised it. And, as Kathleen Tynan points out, he was equally forceful when he took on the post of *dramaturg* for the National Theatre in what has proved, in retrospect, to be its formative period, before it got its own building.

Olivier, the man in charge, emerges from this book like the giant he was and is, but it is to Tynan's lasting credit that when the man was matched with his hour, he, Tynan, was a match for the man. In service of Olivier, all of Tynan's knowledge, judgment and love of the theatre were put to good use.

So where was the vice? It was in the virtue. He loved theatre so much that he thought life should be like that. It was not his trendiness that caught up with him in the 1960s, it was his seriousness. His late-flowering admiration for Brecht might not have been fatal if he had abetted it by some capacity for political analysis. But he tried to learn politics *from* Brecht. Tynan's evocations of

86

the Berliner Ensemble productions (to be found in his collection 'Curtains') are alive in all respects except the intellect. He didn't think to ask why Brecht's company had never been invited to tour the Soviet Union, or why Brecht himself had never written a single line, let alone a complete play, in direct criticism of any aspect of the East German regime. He could be so foolish only because he had failed to take history in. It was too dull for him.

Tynan had read every play in the world but very few serious books. There was no time. He dined in smart company almost every night. He lived the high life and could not bear to be away from it. He could have conquered his emphysema if he had kept to the desert air, but it would have wasted his sweetness. He had to be near the action – not because he was a snob, but because it was theatrical. The entrance on to the stage of Olivier as Othello was succeeded by the entrance into the dining-room of Princess Margaret. For Ken Tynan, these events were comparable.

If Kathleen Tynan seems to think the same, the sin is more venial in her than it was in her husband. She has some innocent pleasure coming, after the pain he caused her, her worst pain arising from the requirement that she should witness his. No wonder she looks for a profound cause of why he fell to pieces. Without making light of the bewilderment he brought to his women and children, however, it should be possible to conjecture that he disintegrated for the same reason that a meteor does, which consumes itself in order to be brilliant, and presumably wouldn't, if consulted, choose another course. To want an unfallen Kenneth Tynan would be to want the moon.

Observer
27 September, 1987

For Terence Kilmartin

(An address read at his memorial service in the Stationers'
Hall on October 28th, 1991)

FOR HOW but in custom and in ceremony are innocence
and beauty born? That idea always seemed right to
me even when I thought I disagreed with it, and now,
tonight, at this ceremony, the thing is proved. If there is
an afterlife then this is it. The only immortality most of us
can realistically hope for is to live on in the minds of our
friends, and those of us with less expectation of a crowded
graveside have already had good cause to be envious this
evening, seeing how many people have come from so far to
bring their memories of you together. You're here if you're
anywhere, and on behalf of all the awkward beginners you
once helped to shepherd I say my piece straight to you,
knowing that in your life, in my case, it was the whole-
hearted blunder, the truly clueless *bêtise*, that you relished.

On the surface you were a keeper of secrets, a
Richelieu or a Mazarin, a pillar of the cultural Establishment. Underneath you were an Irish hell-raiser, the
kind of rapscallion you fondly characterised as the 'desperate chancer', the only London literary editor of modern
times to have *done* time in a French gaol. You liked nothing
more than to see a bull run loose in the china shop, partly
because you realised better than anyone that Grub Street,
if it was to live at all, had to be something less specialised,
less delicate, than a china shop. Your justly celebrated
integrity was far beyond being just a taste for decorum.
You enjoyed seeing the thing that was not done done,
unless you thought it was wrong. If you thought it was
wrong you objected on principle. Everyone courted your
delighted smile. Nobody wanted your disapproval. I don't

want it now, and still don't write a line without imagining
you reading it, either with the barely detectable snort that
meant amusement, or the sideways look across the top of
the half-glasses which meant that something had to come
out.

Everyone who ever had his copy edited by you
has a story like mine and probably better, but here
and now, for them, is my chance to tell you what it was
actually like to have written a book review for you and
to have described what was really quite a good novel as
'hugely impressive'. Holding the offending page of foolscap,
you looked sideways across the top of your half-glasses and
said 'Do you *really* want to say that?' I'm leaving out your
ums and ahs, which I'm certain were a way of putting
your interlocutor on the spot: they were your version of a
pub-fighter's pre-emptive head-butt to leave his opponent
stunned. 'Do you really,' you went on, 'do you *really* want
to say *hugely* impressive? What's wrong with just *impressive*?'
I said I thought the book was better than just impressive.
You said 'How about *very* impressive, then?' I said that
didn't sound impressive enough – it sounded like a cliché.
You said 'But surely if you *qualify* the word 'impressive'
you *make* it sound like a cliché, don't you? I mean, good
God, either the word 'impressive' on its own means you're
impressed, or you need another word *instead*. But I should
have thought the last thing you need is another word *as
well*.' I said OK, take out the hugely. You said 'I think
we're doing the right thing, don't you?' I said 'Take it *out*,
take it *out*!' Finally persuaded, you lifted your pencil and
softly struck.

I rarely thought you overdid it with my copy. I
did think you sometimes overdid it with other people's, especially when they were praising my books. My
first book, pompously entitled *The Metropolitan Critic*, was
extravagantly praised by your then chief reviewer Philip
Toynbee. As the *Observer*'s new TV columnist I had access
to your office and managed to see Toynbee's piece before
you did. It was full of superlatives which I thought well
judged and objective. That night in the pub I told my

friends and several strangers that my first book was about to be warmly received in my own newspaper. When the piece was published all the superlatives were gone. I got the impression that there was nothing left except a few prepositions and a brief physical description of the book's size and weight. I blamed you for a long time. I could see why Caesar's wife had to be above suspicion but I couldn't see why Caesar's son had to be beyond praise. I thought myself hard done by.

Actually you had taught me the lesson that you went on teaching to anyone who showed signs of needing to learn it: no favours, or even the appearance of them. The generation of writers you taught are nowadays often accused by the next generation coming up of rolling logs for each other and taking in each other's washing. The truth is that they hardly ever do; not just because each is properly jealous of his reputation for independence but because they all remember what your anger was like at any hint of collusion. It was a variation on the low-pressure snort, but without the smile. When a well-connected first-time novelist once started phoning around to engineer an easy ride for her fledgling creation, it was the only time I ever saw you angry with a woman.

Your office was a university but you were an even better teacher out of school. One evening at your house in Chelsea I was banging on about how the newly rediscovered *Les Troyens* of Berlioz would never be popular because the good bits were even further apart than in Wagner and, let's face it, Berlioz wrote terrific memoirs but he couldn't finish a tune. While I was talking you changed the music on the stereo and we were gently assaulted by a melody of such beauty that even I drew breath. 'What the Hell is *that*?' I asked, dead on cue as always in my role in your life as the man whose foot had gone soft from the amount of time it spent in his mouth. 'Régine Crespin,' you said. 'Singing what?' I said. '*Les Nuits d'été*,' you said. 'But who *wrote* it?' I said. 'Um, ah, Berlioz.'

You pulled the same trick with Raymond Aron,

whose books I had discovered after realising that anyone so consistently disparaged by Sartre must be all right.
Incidentally, there's a book just come out in France which
convincingly demonstrates that the heroic Resistance activities of Sartre and de Beauvoir were entirely imaginary.*
I think you'd enjoy it, although as a man who really *did*
risk his life for a free France you were always slow to
condemn those who only pretended to. Perhaps there was
another lesson there. Anyway, I had discovered Raymond
Aron and read all his major works, even the heavy, multi-
volume stuff like the treatise on nuclear war. French is a
language I find it hard to speak but love to read. Even
though you spoke it perfectly you always encouraged me
to go on reading. You were absolutely without intellectual
snobbery but I thought you were being a bit *too* much of
the anti-Establishment rebel when you warned me against
Aron's conservatism. I cited chapter and verse from *L'opium
des intellectuels* to prove that Aron was merely a sound social
democrat. You said that you were a bit out of touch with
all that by now and I might well be right. Months later I
saw in a second-hand bookshop an English translation of
the very book I had quoted at you. It looked as if it dated
from about twenty years back. I thought it would make a
good crib if the translator had been up to reproducing the
transparency of Aron's French. I opened the book to see
who the translator was. *The Opium of the Intellectuals*, by
Raymond Aron. Translated by Terence Kilmartin.

Any other man would have won the argument at the
time, by pulling rank. Most of us need to prove ourselves from day to day. You had done it before most
of us met you. It was the reason why so quiet a man
could have such authority. Every man's admiration for
you had an edge of soul-searching, and Joanna won't
mind my saying that no woman who laid eyes on you
ever doubted that you were the Truly Strong Man. The
phrase was coined by Auden and it was meant to make
us think of some bare-chested Horst model in a pilot's

*Gilbert Joseph, *Une si douce Occupation*, Paris, 1991.

helmet climbing F-6 with a pickaxe, but it makes a lot of us think of you: as heterosexual as they come yet still the perfect go-between for Proust. You were masculine without assertion, sympathetic without intrusion, modest without subservience, charming without limit. Your pride in your profession was fierce and in your status non-existent. You had stature instead, and must have known it, but that didn't show either. Your good looks never spoiled you for the cruel reality of the rolling dice and when pain came you were a Stoic. We who remain would like to think that we are stoic too but would prefer a version that didn't hurt. We would prefer a life from which you were not gone. But your influence is alive and will last for a long time, passed on to the young ones as an example and a name: the name of a hugely impressive – all right, an impressive – man we once met, and who is all ours now.

Pit-bull Poodle

A N EXPLOSION of interest in the subject of Australian republicanism reverberated around the world last week. Grizzled expatriates who thought they were safely holed up in this country were shaken to their foundation garments. There was no dodging the issue. Some said it was the first eruption of a long-simmering volcano. Others thought a squib had gone off. The initial evidence supported the latter theory. Meeting the Queen during her tour of Australia, the Australian Prime Minister's wife had several times failed to curtsy, while the Prime Minister himself, on at least one occasion, had physically touched the Monarch, at at least one point.

For a while it was not established whether these were deliberate acts of *lèse-majesté* or examples of disarming Australian casualness. But the prominent British art critic, Brian Sewell, was already certain. The *Evening Standard* ran a full-page article from him recommending that all Australian expatriates in Britain should be deported back to their inherently treasonable country.

My own name was high on the list, with a full description. I reacted with some alarm. Though Auberon Waugh once made the same suggestion, he had been talking about voluntary repatriation, like Enoch Powell. Brian Sewell's tone was less kindly. I had always thought he sounded like a decorative attack dog, a sort of pit-bull poodle, but this time he was really barking. Those British cultural journalists of the second rank who enjoy baiting Australians as a form of licensed racism had previously worn muzzles. Brian Sewell gave you a taste of what it must have been like to be Jewish in Nazi-occupied Paris when Brasillach was writing for *Je suit partout*. First the denunciation, then they wake you up during the night.

Sleeping that night with my passport in my pyjama pocket I was woken early by a telephone call from the *Evening Standard*. Quelling the urge to answer in a disguised voice and exit backwards through the bedroom window, I bravely asked them what they wanted. It turned out that Prime Minister Keating, responding in Parliament to a taunt about his behaviour *vis-à-vis* the Monarch, had condemned Britain's shameless indifference to Australia's fate during the Second World War. Would I care to comment? I told them to ask Brian Sewell.

There was no getting out of it that easily. Over the next few days *Newsnight*, *The World At One* and most of the newspapers were all on the trail. Everyone wanted my expert opinion on the Australian constitutional issue. Did I *look* like an expert on the Australian constitutional issue? I tried on a false beard, but it made me look like Tom Keneally, who *is* an expert on the Australian constitutional issue. He is in favour of an Australian republic. I'm not, but I'm not sure why. To get out of having to dodge any more questions, however, let me give the few answers in my possession.

Paul Keating is a man of conspicuous virtues. He has a nice line in vituperation which could have made him a successful debt collector in another life. When the moment came to pull the lever which dropped Mr Hawke through the trap-door to the waiting crocodiles, Mr Keating did not pretend to share their tears. His boldness is proved by the unblushing confidence with which he now proposes to rebuild a national economy that all Australians, including possibly himself, are well aware he destroyed in the first place. He will probably make a good, long-serving prime minister in the not impossible event that the opposition remains so short of credible leadership it can't beat even him.

But he knows nothing about the modern history of Australia or anywhere else. He left school early and has too readily excused himself from making up his educational deficiencies late at night. Instead of reading English books, he collects French clocks, which can tell him nothing except the time. Compared to most of his predecessors as leader of the Labor Party, he is an ignoramus. Dr H. V. Evatt might be said to have been privileged, because he went to Sydney University and had a dazzling academic record; and Bob Hawke was even more privileged, because he went to Oxford University and drank beer; but Ben Chifley, though his school was the footplate of a locomotive, found out about the world by asking. Paul Keating doesn't ask. He can't be instructed because he is always instructing. Tempted out of his field, which is bare-knuckle politics, he finds himself compelled to relay, as a substitute for what he has found out from experience, stuff he has got out of the air. What is of interest is not his belligerence but how the stuff got into the air.

As Alistair Horne made clear, when the British posh papers wheeled him into the argument, the idea that Britain deliberately did less than it could to save Malaya, Singapore, and finally Australia, has no basis in fact. It shouldn't have needed Mr Horne to point this out. Republican-minded Australian revisionist historians have been able to float the notion only by blinding themselves to the obvious. The Malaya campaign was a bungle which cost Britain dear, and if there were any plans by Britain to abandon Australia, they were scarcely more sweeping than Australian plans to do the same. Planning against the worst is a military necessity. When the Australians counted up their resources they had to face the possibility that if the Japanese got ashore the only defensible perimeter would be the eastern seaboard: 'the Brisbane line'. This proposal, which was drawn up in some detail, is no reason for the inhabitants of Adelaide and Perth to now demand a separate country of their own. Luckily the American navy fought a crucial draw with the Japanese navy at the Battle of the Coral Sea and the Australian army stymied the Japanese army in New Guinea, so the prospect of abandoning Australia ceased to loom. But it might have happened, because it might have had to.

The Australians showed more resentment for the

Americans who came to their rescue than for the British who had been so ineffective in defending the Empire. The idea that Australians *should* have borne ill-will towards Britain was hatched subsequently by revisionist historians with an interest in republicanism. It is a legitimate interest, especially in view of Britain's undoubted indifference to the sensitivities of Australia and New Zealand at the time of its belated entry into the Common Market. But to play fast and loose with the truth in order to further a political interest is not legitimate, and nothing is more likely to make Australia go on seeming provincial than this propensity on the part of its artists and intellectuals to tinker with ideology. You can understand it from the Murdoch press. Its proprietor favours Australia cutting itself off from Britain because he has cut himself off from both countries, in pursuit of some dreary post-capitalist Utopia in which the hunger to acquire is exalted as a spiritual value, and the amount of debt magically testifies to financial acumen. But there is no good reason why some of Australia's most creative people should share his bleak vision.

And yet they do. In Australia the conspiracy theory of history wins in a walk and the cock-up theory comes nowhere. At the Dardanelles three times as many British troops were uselessly thrown into the same boiler as the Australians, but the fact doesn't get a mention in the Australian-made film *Gallipoli* because its writer, David Williamson, favours a republic. Williamson is a gifted man who must know the truth. But he has an end in view. The conspiracy theory that Britain cynically exploited Antipodean cannon-fodder in both wars is seen to further this end.

I wonder if it will. Ordinary Australian people, less bound by the requirements to write a neat article or a clear-cut screenplay, are more likely to favour the cock-up theory, especially if they are old enough actually to remember what the war in the Pacific was like. Indeed, some of them might be inclined to extend that theory to a full-blown view of the world's contingencies, one of them being that if the British had done everything right in Malaya, they might still have lost.

It is racism of a particularly insidious kind to imagine that the Japanese were able to advance only because we retreated. General Percival, commanding for Britain, was certainly no genius, but even if he had been Montgomery and Slim rolled into one he would have had trouble with General Yamashita, a strategic prodigy in command of an army which comported itself brilliantly all the way down to platoon level. After the fall of Singapore, Yamashita was banished to Mongolia by a jealous Tojo, but with the war almost lost he was brought back to stop the rot on Luzon, where the Americans, by then wielding limitless resources, found to their horror that his troops had to be cooked out of their holes, and came out shooting even when they were burning.

Mr Keating's assumption that a modernised, Asia-minded Australia must necessarily be a republic might be greeted with some puzzlement by present-day Japan, whose economic clout dominates the region and whose Emperor, at his coronation, spent a night in the embrace of the Sun Goddess. Mr Keating's real problem, however, is with my mother. Though fiercely proud to be Australian, she has made a point of seeing with her own eyes all the officially visiting members of the Royal Family since the present Queen Mother was the Duchess of York. When the present Queen first visited Sydney in 1954, my mother came in by train to wave. She was there again for the Queen's visit this year. The two women are very like each other, sharing the same past, if not the same income. My mother did not, and does not now, regard my father's death as a pointless sacrifice on behalf of British interests. She believes that he was defending civilisation. Though Mr Menzies took care to keep her war widow's pension small so as to encourage thrift, she voted for the Liberal Party as often as for Labor, and always according to her assessment of which party had the firmer grip on reality. She has personally elected every Australian prime minister for the last sixty years and if Mr Keating thinks he can do without her vote, it might be his turn on the trap-door.

Nor should he put too much faith in the argument – much touted by the Murdoch press and slyly put forward as fact by the Australian broadcaster Mike Carlton in his entertaining article in the *Sunday Times* – that as Australia's demography alters to put people of Anglo background in the minority, the majority are bound to prefer going it alone. Whether from Europe two generations ago or from Asia in the last generation, many of Australia's migrants were refugees from political instability, and won't necessarily favour any proposal that encourages more of it in their chosen home. Their progeny might be persuaded, but let it be by reasonable argument, on a basis of truth. Meanwhile for Australians like myself, resident in Britain but still holding on loyally to their Australian passports, caught between Mr Sewell and Mr Keating, queueing in the 'Other Passports' channel while ex-SS tank commanders are given the quick welcome reserved for the EEC, there is nothing to do but wait, and screen all incoming calls.

Spectator
7 March, 1992

Part Two:

THE POLITICS OF TELEVISION

The Words Count

(Opening address to the IBA Consultation on Entertainment Programmes, Cheltenham, February, 1986)

F ACING SO many highly qualified administrators, controllers, department heads and deep thinkers, I must begin by saying that I admire your strategy. By asking someone as unqualified as I am to deliver an opening address, you give yourselves something to agree on. You all know a lot about the organisation that lies behind television, and in the next few days of discussion your knowledge will inevitably lead to disagreements, the facts being intractable, the interpretation of them personal, and personalities divergent. But for now you can unite for an hour in showing expansive tolerance for someone who does not know what he is talking about. I am fairly certain that that is why I was chosen. What little I know about television I have learned from watching the set or else appearing within its framework. I have looked at it and I have been on it, but I have never run it.

I will not flatter myself by saying that I lack the appetite for power. Nobody who actually says that should ever be believed. But I do lack the qualifications for it. For an Australian to exercise power in the media today, he must have military qualities. He must have the ability to fortify a large building in the East End of London and to defend it against even the most ferocious woman trade union leader. He must know how to string barbed-wire and booby-trap a doorway so that even the most inquisitive journalist is unable to get out. He must have the organisational talent of Eisenhower, the tactical audacity of Rommel, the self-justifying eloquence of Montgomery and the operational flexibility of Roland

Rat. I do not pretend to possess these gifts. The internal politics of the business has never been my bailiwick. In my ten years as a television critic I never met anybody except in the form of an image about eight inches high. I think I only ever went to one preview. It was in Golden Square, and when Sir Denis Forman offered me a sandwich I asked him how long he had been with the catering company.

In my later capacity as a performer, mainly for LWT, I have learned to tell John Birt from Brian Tesler, and recently at Kent House I have quite often met either or both of them in the lift, but when I get off at the fourteenth floor I have no idea where they go next. Maybe they go all the way up to see Melvyn Bragg. Maybe they keep going straight on up out of the top of the building. Perhaps they go back down to the basement and go home. All I know about what they do is that I could not do it. They are welcome to their end of the business, which depends on a broad understanding of the big picture. That the big picture is on such a small screen only makes the comprehension of it a more taxing challenge. It is a challenge which I am temperamentally incapable of meeting. I am not just poor-mouthing myself on this point. As a critic, I think I was capable of spotting specific things which my more generalising colleagues missed. Regarding the Barbara Woodhouse programmes about dog-training, for example, I was the first critic to notice that those dog-owners who did not follow her instructions disappeared from the next episode. And I solved the mystery of where they had gone by noting how the dogs had got fatter.

But these and similar perceptions I arrived at without developing a capacity to theorise. One tries not to be too ashamed of this. It could be said that some minds are so clear in their imaginative workings that the faculty of ratiocination is precluded. T. S. Eliot – during the short time that he was working as a Channel 4 commissioning editor – said of Henry James that he had a mind so fine that no idea could violate it. Nobody ever said that about the mind of Clive James except the deputy headmaster of Sydney Technical High School in 1956. But I prefer to think that the evidence all points that way. Nevertheless, the glaring fact that in a decade of television criticism I never contributed even one theory to the flourishing field of abstract media studies still nags me. It was one of the most embarrassing hours of my life – even more embarrassing than this one could well turn out to be – when Lord Annan, while gathering learned opinions for his famed report, received me at University College, London in private session for a working lunch: just him and me and a small roll-mop salad each. He asked me what I thought of television in general. I just could not come up with even one general observation. He looked at his sagging roll-mop as a peer of the realm will who realises that he has just blown his lunch-hour. We have remained friends ever since but only on the understanding that we discuss Lytton Strachey or Virginia Woolf. The subject of television never comes up, because we both remember too well that, apart from a few specific objections, I had nothing to say except that I was on the whole grateful for how the medium was managed in Britain and hoped that it would go on roughly as it was. I can just remember recommending that the fourth channel should go to ITV so that the BBC and the IBA could share power equally. I believed in the duopoly. He did, too, and I think most people did. And I think probably they still do, although the exceptions have grown more vociferous. Perhaps they have forgotten how lucky we are; lucky in that British television offers only cause for concern instead of cause for despair. Nobody except a few die-hard academics assumes our television to be a write-off. Even its most inquisitorial would-be reformers – in fact, especially them – acknowledge its importance as a shaping force. Everyone knows that television transmits values, whether real, false or confused. It is just that no-one except the over-confident Comstockian witch-finder knows exactly how this transmission of values occurs. For what my own guess is worth, I think television imposes, or at any rate reinforces, cultural values most powerfully when they are least explicitly stated. To put it more specifically, less theoretically, it does not matter so much if a playwright is

narrowly left wing, it matters more if a political commentator is narrowly right wing, and it matters a great deal if the
host of a game show is a racist. It is through entertainment
that television reaches most people and reaches them most
deeply. A performer on *Weekend World* can say with a clear
conscience whatever Brian Walden will let him get away
with, but a performer on a prime-time entertainment show
should watch his words. The words count.

Game shows are for me the least congenial area of
entertainment, but even about those I find it hard to
get worked up into the belief that civilisation as we know it
is on its way down the tubes through the tube. If this were
America, I might have some spleen to vent on the subject
and might even write my version of *Amusing Ourselves to
Death*, a book which in the US gets published every five
years or so, with a different author and title but the same
argument and predictable press reaction. Here, I doubt if
we are amusing ourselves to death even with our mentally
least nutritious programming, and I suppose game shows
come under that heading. Even in America, it is an open
question whether the worst game show is more culturally
damaging than, say, gladiatorial game shows were for
Augustan Rome or bear-baiting for Elizabethan England. I
will leave aside the question of game shows in Japan, except
to repeat the rhetorical question I have already asked when
summing them up on screen: if a Japanese producer's idea
of a good show is to stuff the contestants' plastic knickers
full of live cockroaches while they hang upside down over
a slow fire, what would you rather he was doing instead?
Would you rather he was in the army? In the air force, perhaps? Japanese game shows are the most obvious instance
of television catering for impulses which might be lethal if
not expressed in playful form. The possibility that *The Price
Is Right* is doing the same thing should not be dismissed
lightly.

As for our worst game shows, they are usually
imported versions of America's second-worst game
shows. My younger daughter loves them, and I cannot see
how that passion is destroying her character, her reading

skills or her reason. I will not bend over backwards any
further than that lest I be suspected of trying to soothe one
of my current employers, LWT's Alan Boyd, a game-show
scientist who will be telling you all about what lies ahead
in that field of achievement. The simple fact is that I
hardly ever watch any programme involving questions
and answers unless Joanna Lumley is on the panel. But
the simple fact arises less from moral disapproval than from
irrational aversion, probably traumatic. When *New Faces*
started up, I was cast as the heavy critic on the panel, the
man who told the pitiless truth about the talent on display.
After the first, locally transmitted pilot, I was generally held
to be a success at this, one of the contestants having burst
into tears on screen. After the second, nationally transmitted pilot, I was offered a glittering contract. But I had come
to the moment of truth during that second programme,
when a singing weightlifter, preparatory to giving us his
rendition of 'My Way', put an empty hot-water bottle to
his pursed lips and blew it up until it burst. Before that
obscene salmon-pink membrane had even finished swelling
– he disappeared behind it like a pup behind a television
pouffe – I already knew that I would have to make a
decision about what kind of television I wanted to do. I
made that decision and walked away from it for ever: the
chauffeured limo, the Havana cigars, the swimming-pool,
everything that Michael Parkinson holds dear.

But I do not believe that Parkinson or Michael
Aspel or Robert Robinson or Bruce Forsyth or Leslie
Crowther or anyone who conducts a game or a panel show
in a considerate, responsible way is wasting his time. There
is a line to be drawn and on the whole British television has
drawn it and stays on the right side of it. The American
game shows are greedy not just in money terms but in
how they rob their own air-time of precious reality. By
coaching the public to become performers they commit a
small but real crime against humanity. We still allow the
contestants to be unreconstructed human beings, and our
hosts, if not as unreconstructed as they might be, are at
least not androids on the American model. Some of our

chaps wear wigs, but the wigs are not made of Teflon: they crackle when touched but do not glow in the dark.

A game show is light entertainment and nothing else, so it might seem a minor point to keep it human. But that is what makes it a major point. Millions of people are watching, at their least critical, their most defenceless. The host should be an identifiable member of *Homo sapiens*, capable of treating people in a civil manner and of saying a few things of his own, not just cranking out special material. Even in game shows, the words count. We want to hear the human voice, not just patter. Otherwise, Max Headroom might as well take over. He could, of course: if the computer controls the controller, and the bottom line becomes the only line, you could program the whole programme.

In situation comedy, that would be more difficult, because in situation comedy the public loves the actor. When the audience thinks of *Porridge*, it thinks of Fletch, and of Ronnie Barker as Fletch. When the public thinks of *Auf Wiedersehen, Pet*, it thinks not just of the characters but of those actors being those characters. Hence the sadness that tinged the delight of seeing the first episode of the new series of *Auf Wiedersehen, Pet*, knowing that one of the actors had died an untimely death.

Many commentators about television bewail the audience's supposed inability to tell the actor from the character, and indeed there is something worrying about how the Fleet Street tabloids encourage readers to get Joan Collins mixed up with Alexis. But I think the confusion probably lies more in Fleet Street's motives than in the public's responses. People know that their favourite sitcom characters are not *really* real. They enjoy appreciating them *as if* they were real. What the public does not know and cannot know, however – what even some of the younger actors concerned do not yet know but will find out when they move on to a less rewarding show – is how important the writing is, how much the words count.

Good scripts sound effortless, as if they grew on trees. But as I do not need to tell you, of all people, they are made, and only with great effort, and are a lot rarer than gold. Several years ago Russell Harty took me to a secret meeting with a BBC controller at Broadcasting House. LWT never knew I was at that meeting, and I would not want them to think I was leaking the information now just because contract time is coming up, but the story is too illustrative to leave out. The BBC controller, who must now be nameless – come to think of it, he was pretty nameless then – complained that he was ready to pay anything for another series of *Fawlty Towers* but John Cleese and Connie Booth could not be persuaded. In other words, there was a force in these things which was more powerful than money. It was, of course, creativity. A good sitcom, we agreed, grew from inspiration and therefore must have its natural term. We all agreed about this while washing down the game pie with an excellent claret. The lunch was taking place in one of those BBC *chambre séparée* executive dining-roomettes furnished with left-over fittings from a pre-war Atlantic liner. We were discussing the importance of transcending materialist values while eating the equivalent of two licence fees.

But the principle remains true. The sitcoms that reach the nation's heart are written from that same organ. They are matters of calculation only in the second instance. In the first instance they are done from love. It is a point worth remembering when you wonder how to get Clement and La Frenais to come up with the same goods as before. There they are in Los Angeles, sitting around their swimming-pool, or in their twin jacuzzis, listlessly making another million by rewriting their own script for a movie whose profitability depends on its never actually being made. How can you raise enough scratch to tempt them back home to write *Porridge* again? You can't. There isn't enough money. But they *will* write *Auf Wiedersehen, Pet*, because to them it is an adventure, something new they want to do. And when they do, the results are so much better than they need to be that it makes you wonder. In the theatre, a radical playwright can build a giant reputation for political relevance while having scarcely half the verbal talent of either Clement or La Frenais taken separately, let alone together. But the important thing to remember is that he has not got half the political relevance, either. Alan Bleasdale is an obvious case of a writer who manages to impose a sophisticated political view through apparently naïve means. Jay and Lynn in *Yes, Minister* are a less obvious example, since their view is more like what most of us believe and so does not strike us as a peculiar vision. But in every case the television writer who becomes a name is giving us a personal view. Even Eddie Braben, when he wrote for Morecambe and Wise, gave us a view uniquely his. It was one of the things that made them them.

What makes the personal view strike home to the viewer, however, is the sense of reality that comes with it. The unique writers have that in common. It is not a paradox, or not meant to sound like one, to say that that is what makes them unique: what they have in common. They make us feel: yes, our life is like that, at least in part. And it is the sense of community which results from that kind of entertainment which makes British television valuable above the level of mere commerce. A sure sign of how deep this community spirit runs is that the television companies have so far persevered in the uneconomically painstaking task of seeking out the kind of writing talent which makes it possible. I hope the search goes on, even if it means publicly acknowledging what Hollywood has never had the courage to admit: the crucial importance of the writer. The words count.

Somebody once said that talent is rare but the talent to handle talent is rarer still. I am sure that is true. First you have to get Verity Lambert, and then she has to get Linda Agran, and only then do you get *Minder*. The writer might possibly have got the project off the ground on his own, but it would crash at the end of the runway. It takes a common effort to make good on even the best ideas. A company that looks after its sitcom writers, giving them a home to go to, letting their new projects mature at the proper rate, is a company that is doing more than it needs to do for itself in the short term. It is looking to the long term on behalf of the whole country, and one sincerely trusts that such efforts are noticed when the time comes to award or re-award or take away franchises.

I might also say that the fourth channel seems to me to be the ideal place for an initially audacious sitcom idea to find its feet before moving to the third channel and the mass audience. The BBC, in however slapdash a manner, has already used its two channels to some advantage in this regard, and, if a certain BBC 1 controller with contact lenses and sharp socks ever gets his hands on both outlets, he is likely to use BBC 2 for out-of-town try-outs, BBC 1 for a West End run, pick up a profit both ways and appear on an LWT talk show to tell us how he did it.*

But here again I have no publishable theories about how things could be better. I continue to be startled by how good things are. The best British television sitcoms are a blessing we have no right to expect. They are thought of as a blessing in Australia too, incidentally, where they run mainly on ABC Television and remind the delighted viewers of their loyalty: loyalty not so much to the Crown – some of the viewers might be republicans – but loyalty to the language. The words count.

When it comes to pure comedy shows, my stress on the importance of writing would have seemed, until very recent times, supererogatory. Everyone who has ever suffered through a wedding reception while the best man tries to save a bad speech with funny faces knows that the script is vital; everyone except journalists, who would rather tell a simple story about one person than a complex one about a collaboration. Hence once again we get a *Radio Times* cover story calling Tony Hancock the greatest British comedian since the war, because that is an easier story to write than the one about the confused man with questionable judgment who was the greatest British comedian since the war, but only when he was temporarily smart enough to realise that Galton and Simpson were donating his life's blood.

*At this time Michael Grade was controller of BBC 1.

The well-founded tradition that good comedy must first be created on the page before the comedian can body it forth on stage or screen still remains strong, even if not well understood by cultural commentators. Victoria Wood is a heartening example of a writer and performer all rolled into one person whose sense of structure would be saluted by Muir and Norden as something either would have to think for a bit before matching on his own. In her material she mentions what would once have been unmentionable, yet she does so in a disciplined way, working that difficult trick – which is the writer's trick – of establishing a climate of tolerance just ahead of the advancing outrage.

But while the written comic tradition continues in the best British manner, there has been one significant break in it, and the break breaks both ways. The break is alternative comedy. Let me personalise this issue immediately by declaring that I was practically the last person in Britain to hear about alternative comedy, after the Archbishop of Canterbury and only just ahead of the Queen. I was a guest one night on the BBC's *Friday Night and Saturday Morning*. It was a show on which they changed the host more often than the guests, so it never really settled in, but I went on it for the usual high-minded reason: i.e. I wanted to sit back on a deep sofa with Lesley-Anne Down. In between some only fitfully scintillating stretches of conversation there were interludes purporting to offer comic relief. These numbers were direly unfunny except for an act called Twentieth Century Coyote, which turned out to be two young men, one of whom was Rik Mayall. I laughed until a valve burst and quizzed them afterwards on their background. What a relief to find that they had nothing to do with Cambridge Footlights. I do not want to sound disloyal to the dear old club, because I owe to it my own beginnings in the British media, a hard field for an Australian to crack unless he has Joan Sutherland's voice, Barry Humphries' high heels, Olivia Newton-John's pink gums or Germaine Greer's shy charm. But the Oxbridge connection had dominated theatrical revue and its television offshoots far too thoroughly and for far too long, and, although I did not want to see this influence entirely replaced, I could not repress a yell of glee at seeing it supplemented. Alternative comedy told us more about the state of the nation. The communal sense of life as it is actually lived came through with renewed strength. That was a clear gain. What struck me at the time as a potential loss, however, and now begins to strike me as an actual loss, was the use of language. And by that I mean bad language: badly written bad language.

They did swear a lot, and later on, when the demand for fresh ideas started to outrun the supply, they swore even more. One of my very few theories about anything concerns swearing. Actually, the theory is just a restatement of the law of diminishing returns. By using bad language habitually, you may or may not lose your audience, but you must eventually lose your capacity to swear. You cannot say 'shit' all the time and still hope to say 'shit' for effect. You cannot shock if you are shocking all the time. All you can do is bore. For a sharp weapon to keep its edge, it must spend most of its life in the scabbard.

It is with circumspection, trepidation and what humility I can muster that I take this line. It might just be that I have been outdistanced by events. Perhaps the best way to cope with the allegedly irredeemable squalor of life in modern Britain is not just to comment on its ugliness but to mimic its accent; to fill the screen with the litter in the streets, the graffiti in the stairwell. If the young men on the football terraces mangle the English language, let the young presenters on the screen mangle the English language too. The case for realism is always stronger, or anyway more easily stated, than the case for stylisation. The young want to be involved, and when the old say that the only way to stay involved is to sound detached the young are right to distrust them, because it smacks of sophistry, and often is. Also, this is perhaps a bad time to suggest limits, when you consider who else is not only suggesting limits but demanding their imposition.

It was written in the stars that Mary Whitehouse and Winston Churchill should one day get together. One only hopes that their union will be blessed with offspring. They could start a whole new human race with none of the failings of the present one. Having met Mrs Whitehouse at an occasion a bit like this – it was a conference of the Royal Television Society held at King's College, Cambridge – like all men present I was ravished by the metallic sheen of her hair arrangement and the vitreous portcullis of her smile, but I wondered what on earth she was doing there among all those BBC bigwigs. Why had they invited her, if she was challenging their authority? And why had she accepted the invitation, if she thought they were incompetent?

The prominence of young Winston is rather more easily explained. He first sprang to my attention when he tried to stop a couple of geriatric ex-SS officers visiting Britain. Obviously he had heard that it was traditional for someone called Winston Churchill to stop German officers visiting England. His moral position with regard to these doddering old killers was impeccable, but it was noticeable that his way of dealing with something unpalatable was not to look at it, and to stop anyone else looking at it, too. No surprise, then, that he and Mrs Whitehouse would be pushing less for a prescriptive list of what should be shown than for a proscriptive list of what should not – an *index expurgatorium*.

It would be generous to this initiative to call it half-witted. The whole communications establishment has justifiably snorted in derisive unison at the very prospect. But such a clumsy grab for power would not have got this close if it was not heading towards a vacuum. The power vacuum is exemplified by the most fluent defending counsel against censorship, John Mortimer. His piece on the subject in *The Times* put the permissive case, as he always puts it, with bewitching clarity. Our duty, he argues – and I am paraphrasing here, but I hope not falsifying – is to reflect life as it is and to stave off those who would put restrictions on our freedom to do so.

John Mortimer is a great champion of the liberal spirit, and I want to be on his side if I can, but there is a point he has missed. Somebody has to limit us in our urge to reflect life, and, if we do not want someone else to do it, we had better make sure that we do it. We can call it censorship, or we can call it just good taste, or a sense of fitness, but one way and another we have to ensure that not just anything is said. You cannot believe in the power of words, you cannot believe that the words count, and simultaneously hold that anything can be said, at any time, by anyone.

If I can reminisce again – lurching back along what already seems to be the dark corridor of a long career – there was a time about ten years ago when I went up to Manchester to do a spot on a doomed little pop music show for Granada. My first television programmes had been done for Granada: 39 editions of *Cinema*, written and presented for £60 a show plus train fare each way and dinner and breakfast at the Midland Hotel, with a chance to catch a fleeting glimpse of Bamber Gascoigne. I had never got over the heady romance of all that, and when I was asked to do the pop show spot I went back to the North to catch a taste of that old Granadaland thrill again: the long journey and the short contract, the sheer impossibility of getting a drink within the building. Some of you will remember the route to the nearest pub that twisted circuitously behind walls and obstacles so you could not be observed from executive windows. It was called the Ho Chi Minh trail. Here was responsible, sober British television at its most venerable: more decorous than the BBC, less frivolous than the Church of England, as ethically unimpeachable as the Marks & Spencer's staff superannuation scheme.

Into this hallowed context fell a poisonous new pop group called the Sex Pistols. They were the number that I had to follow on the show. It was the first television programme this or any other punk band had ever done. In the Green Room between rehearsal and taping, the Sex Pistols physically attacked everyone in sight, and finally they started attacking each other. As Johnny Rotten fell to the carpet with his yellow teeth sunk in his own shoulder, I congratulated them on the authenticity of their acting. It never occurred to me they were in earnest until they threatened not to go on. Not to go on, in a show which was doing you a favour by booking you at all, was a gesture so insane as to be worth investigating. Why, I asked, were they threatening not to go on? It was because the girl in the group had been asked by the producer to remove her swastika armband.

Perhaps this requirement had come down from Lord Bernstein himself. Perhaps it did not need to come down from him and had been imposed by an executive who was either interpreting his proprietor's wishes or who simply felt that way himself. It is immaterial. The fact remains that here was a plain case of someone who needed to be stopped from doing something.

The day will inevitably come when the Nazi era passes into history. On the day when nobody who suffered from it is left alive, the twelve-year nightmare will begin assuming the same status as the Thirty Years War, about which we can make what jokes we like. But I doubt that that day has come yet, and it certainly had not come then. The Sex Pistols had a case which, if they could not articulate it themselves, could have been advanced for them by anyone not suffering from their speech impediments. Theirs was a band of protest, rejecting the contemporary world. Nazi insignia was either a sign of rebellion in itself, or else could be regarded as a trinket in comparison with the more recent terrors of a society which condemned young people to the dole queue for no better reason than that they had contrived to emerge from school illiterate, innumerate, sociopathic and terminally addicted to glue fumes. But on this particular day this argument was not allowed to cut any ice. Authority was exercised. The appeal to the *Zeitgeist* was disallowed. Daddy knew best.

And daddy *did* know best. The young lady with the swastika armband was very disappointed, even though it was finally conceded that she would not have to take it off, merely cover it up. This concession was more or less enforced by the discovery, made after close inspection, that the armband was in fact a tattoo. As she sullenly wrapped her swastika in flesh-coloured Elastoplast, she told me she could not see what all the bleeding fuss was about. And upon enquiry it rapidly became clear that she did not know what all the bleeding fuss was about. She could not tell Hitler from a hit single. She knew nothing about him. She thought a concentration camp was where all them Germans went to think. I wonder where she is now? I expect she has got three kids and she is running a launderette in the Mile End Road.

It would not be hard to imagine similar instances, less absurd and therefore more sinister, or things that cannot be done or said on screen. There is a lot that we do not and cannot allow to happen on screen while all those people are watching. But controllers ought to come clean about who does the controlling. It should be clearly, unequivocally, them. A vague attempt to let the spirit of the times carry the can must only result in unwanted offers of assistance from Mrs Whitehouse and Mr Churchill, separately or together. I have heard it said that the authority started to drain out of the BBC when Harold Wilson appointed Lord Hill. However it started, the haemorrhage went on until it reached that depressing point very recently where the man who was supposed to speak for the whole organisation could not summon up the energy to open his mouth. Projects became finished programmes before being turned down. Sometimes they were transmitted and then repudiated. Those in authority, because they had not exercised their authority in good time, had no alternative left except to be authoritarian, which is a different thing.

The independent companies have suffered less from this malaise, but the possibility is always there as long as someone who has been appointed to exercise judgment forfeits his right and neglects his duty to judge what is being said. And since what gets said in the area of entertainment is what most closely corresponds to, and very probably helps form, the actual ethical assumptions of the whole country, what gets said is of real importance, even in the apparently marginal field of comedy. Nobody has ever convinced me that the Monty Python people suffered much damage from being rationed in each episode to a certain number of swear words. The obstacle is often the departure point for inspiration.

None of this means that I did not enjoy last night's rerun of *The Bullshitters* on Channel 4. But one of the things that made it funny was that they were not using just bad language. Some of it was good language, in the sense of being well thought out, well written. If all the writing in shows built around 'Comic Strip'-type teams of alternative comedians was of that standard, one would be a little less weary of the trend, but I do not think it is. Recently the BBC had a new prime-time alternative comedy series, a parody sitcom, which was so dirty my children would not let me watch it, but I snuck upstairs, turned on another set and checked it out. It had no chance of being funny. They had no subject matter except television itself, everyone in the show fancied himself as a writer and they were all saying the first thing that came into their heads. Half the team were ex-Footlights pretending to be alternative comedians. They were catching up with the revolution at the very time it was turning into a new orthodoxy.

For their own sakes, the young comedy teams need to be encouraged – which I suppose is a nice way of saying forced – to think harder about the words. The words count. Every young comedy team wants the Woody Allen contract, the agreement Woody Allen had with United Artists which meant that the studio could not interfere as long as he delivered the goods. But that was the point: he delivered the goods. And I am not sure that all the young ones – I use the term sweepingly to include anyone younger than I am who has had it easier – are delivering the goods. I hasten to add that the young ones who were actually called *The Young Ones* were very creative.

But it is quite possible to be very creative and be a disastrous influence. Monty Python ruined comedy for years to come. Just as abstract art increased the opportunity to paint badly, unstructured comedy increased the opportunity to be unfunny. Any breakthrough achieved by the very talented will be run into the ground by the less talented. It is a law of nature. In fact, it is the second law of thermodynamics.

If they were obliged to work harder at the typewriter,

some of the young comedians might have a career after the inevitable day when the team breaks up. The casualty rate must already be fearful, even though, I suspect, the current economics of television temporarily favour a group of young, relatively low paid semi-unknowns against, say, a Stanley Baxter show in which the cost of the white staircase and diamante-studded fountain is not wholly offset by the savings effected through his playing both Fred Astaire and Ginger Rogers. The young comedians are themselves likely to be undercut in their turn by an ever-increasing number of impersonators, each of whom is a whole cast in himself. And when Max Headroom gets access to the appropriate software he will be able to impersonate everybody, including me. In fact, I am not even here this evening, this is a hologram.

Even the puppets must have something to say for themselves, and not even the *Spitting Image* puppets can be allowed to say just anything. I thought the standard of writing on *Spitting Image* went up after the first series and went down again in the latest series and that by no coincidence it was always dirtier when most obviously desperate. Did they economise on the writing? If I can hazard just one more theoretical formulation, this time concerning televised satirical puppet shows: if, when the roller comes up, the names of the puppeteers outnumber the names of the writers by a factor of two to one or more, watch out.

A more practical observation about television satire, and satire in general, is this: a satirical intention, however sincerely felt, does not supersede the requirements of elementary decency. The *Spitting Image* sketch about Gielgud and Olivier reminiscing was one of the funniest things I have ever seen, partly because the tacit pact of shared humanity linking the satirist with the victim had not been rescinded. But I do wonder about the Princess Margaret puppet sloshing down gin. Is she really like that? If she were, would it not be understandable? What is easy about her position? How could she possibly escape it? Is something being said about the shortcomings of constitutional monarchy? If it is, who is saying it? Come out from behind that puppet, whosoever you are. I suspect you are a second-rate journalist from *Private Eye*, which means you are a third-rate journalist from anywhere else. Even in the most passionately committed satirical programme there is a limit to what can be said, and a producer who does not have to fight for his script all the way to the top – just to the top of the company, I do not mean he should have to fight the IBA as well – should be worried about having that much freedom. He should remember Kant's fable about the dove: the dove who, on being told about air resistance, thought it could fly faster if the air were abolished.

One does not ask for authoritarianism. We do not want to go back to that. I doubt if even Winston Churchill wants to go back to the days of the Lord Chamberlain, unless the post were offered to him. One does not even ask for more authority, just a clear, confident expression of the authority that is there already, and necessarily there. Because nothing except resignation will get you people off the hook. Forty channels or four hundred channels will only mean that the television audience will watch the big four more closely, precisely because they are organisations, making a planned attempt, however fallible, to give a responsible picture of life, so as to promote a reasonable living of life.

It all goes forward gradually. It takes a long time for the *Black and White Minstrel Show* to go away and then another long time before Lenny Henry emerges and starts to do some of the work that has made Bill Cosby so important in the United States – more important than Malcolm X, at least as important as James Baldwin, not dwarfed in importance even by Martin Luther King. Life changes entertainment, and entertainment changes life.

It goes forward gradually and sometimes it goes backwards. I just hate canned or boosted laughter. It steals from the audience. There is more of it all the time, and there ought to be less. But our hope of correcting abuses and making advances lies within the responsible organisation. The idea that a fully deregulated, umpteen-channel television entirely determined by market forces will somehow embody democratic choice is not just a boondoggle, it is a con. It is the sales philosophy of Saatchi and Saatchi masquerading as a political vision. For the advertisers to run television would be for the tail to wag the dog. But I will not venture any further into the realm of macro-economics, where all of you are much more at home than I. It is you that understand why the ratings must come down so that the revenue may go up. I am but a humble, bemused toiler in your vineyard.

This has been a long claim on your attention and possibly on your patience, but, at the risk of making things worse, I want to end by saying something about the sort of programmes which I write and appear in myself. The programmes are documentaries; they are specials about television and films, employing the old Granada *Cinema* formula in which short clips are occasionally allowed to interrupt me talking; and then there are talk shows, pure and apparently simple, although I try to put a bit of writing into those, too. None of these programmes quite fits into the category of entertainment. And that is what I like best about them. They have no category.

In the next few days you will be talking about entertainment as if it were a separate thing. This procedure makes a lot of administrative sense. But it only makes *administrative* sense. For the public, all television is entertainment, even the news. And equally, although this aspect is harder to analyse, all television is news, even the entertainment. With due acknowledgement to John Birt and Alan Boyd of LWT and to Michael Grade and David Bell before them, all of whom have given house-room to the extraordinary Special Programmes Unit of my executive producer, Richard Drewett, it was he who taught me to ask, and has made sure I have gone on asking, two basic questions of any project I cook up. The first question is, 'Will anyone be interested in this?', meaning that if it does not entertain it is a dead duck. And the second question is, 'What are we trying to say?', meaning, the words count. If only television were just pictures. But if it were, you would not be here. It would be all so easy, there would be nothing to discuss.

Serious Brain Operation

IN THE week of my fiftieth birthday, after twenty years spent either writing about or appearing on television, I still wouldn't feel entitled to pronounce on the current state of the medium, if it were not for a certain document which has recently fallen into my hands. This document, I believe, blows the whole debate about British television wide open.

The document is called 'World's First Official *The Sun* NEIGHBOURS Collection Sticker Album PLUS EXTRA FREE POSTER PULL-OUT OF JASON AND KYLIE.' A flimsy pamphlet which describes itself as being 'published by EUROFLASH (Sticker Collections) Ltd', it works on the principle that its purchasers must not only fork out for the album, they must fork out again for the stickers to fill in the blanks.

Apparently there are hundreds of thousands of copies of this sticker album in existence, but I am assured that a completed example, with all its stickers in place, is more valuable than the Mappa Mundi. The precious copy in my possession was discovered in the split-level hutch of one of my daughters after she was taken away to a detox unit where *Neighbours* is forcibly withheld. She had got well beyond the point, standard among addicts, of taping each episode and watching it three extra times. She and her little friends had been found studying wiring diagrams so that they could couple up their VCR machines and go into business bootlegging the *Kylie* video on an industrial basis. My faith that I will one day get my daughter back is unshakeable, but if anything was going to shake it, the 'World's First Official *The Sun* NEIGHBOURS Collection Sticker Album' would be a strong candidate.

'It wasn't long ago,' says the caption for a sticker of

some character called Lucy, 'that she was fighting for her life after a serious brain operation.' Boy, do I know how she feels. The album's solitary ray of hope is that one of the stickers of Craig McLachlan is missing. Craig – statistics overwhelmingly suggest that you won't need to be told this, but I insist on believing that there are still a few normal people out there – plays a character called Henry. Billed as a fabulous specimen of young Australian manhood, Craig has a face whose bottom half consists entirely of bared teeth. Ice-blue eyes shine triumphantly out of the top half. The complete assemblage is surrounded by an eruption of straw stuffing, as if he had just won a bodybuilding competition by ramming his head through the back of an old sofa. There are meant to be seven stickers of Craig, but there are only six. It isn't much of a relief, but it's something.

The relevance of this touching publication to the current debate about British television should be obvious. After making allowances for the various percentages due to the *Neighbours* production company and EUROFLASH (Sticker Collections) Ltd, all the profits go to the *Sun*, whose proprietor is my erstwhile compatriot, Rupert Murdoch. It is very hard to see, then, how Rupert Murdoch can plausibly argue that British television, as currently constituted, is unresponsive to the public. When he contends that British television is not sufficiently led by the market, the only possible answer is: how much harder could the market lead it than it is being led now?

Scientists predict that *Neighbours* will eventually affect the whole world, like the hole in the ozone layer, subjecting the human species to the cerebral equivalent of global warming. Masai warriors want Kylie posters. Elusive Jivaro Indians of the upper Amazon have already been heard, although not seen, singing 'I Should Be So Lucky'. But so far the United States, Rupert Murdoch's great example of a market-led television area, is comparatively *Neighbours*-free. Britain is where the market has spoken loudest. More so even than in its country of origin, in Britain *Neighbours* has a direct connection with its viewers.

They watch it until they pass out. They buy stickers. Mr Murdoch's editors, who sell the stickers, are aware, even if he isn't, that when he talks about British television being out of touch with the times he is talking through his hat.

Mr Murdoch has been talking through his hat for some time on this subject. Most conspicuously, he talked through it when invited to deliver the James McTaggart Memorial Lecture in Edinburgh. As has been insufficiently noted, James McTaggart devoted his life to the sort of public service broadcasting which Mr Murdoch, to the small extent that he understands it, loathes. Inviting Rupert Murdoch to address a serious gathering of television professionals was like inviting Evel Knievel to address a road safety conference. Yet Mr Murdoch was listened to with respect. The British are polite. If the positions had been reversed – if a British tycoon had gone to Australia to tell the locals that their most cherished institutions were an offence to his economic precepts – he would have been instructed to pull his head in.

But all the heroic Australian men from Rod Laver to Merv Hughes, and all the heroic Australian women from Margaret Court to those powerful female warders in *Prisoner: Cell Block H*, have established a climate of opinion in which even the loftiest and most worldly-wise British mandarins are in awe of Australian energy. Like the Roman senators in Cavafy's poem, they wait almost longingly for the barbarians to stride in and shake things up. Rupert Murdoch fills the bill exactly. Like a Goth swaggering around Rome wearing an onyx toilet seat for a collar, he exudes self-confidence. Bleach his thatch and he could even be Jason. Not Jason of the Argonauts: Jason of *Neighbours*, described by the 'World's First Official *The Sun* NEIGHBOURS Collection Sticker Album' in Homeric terms: 'Dishy Jason sparked a stampede among his followers when he visited Britain earlier this year. After all, there's no home-grown talent to compete with those healthy, blond all-Australian looks.'

That's just what Rupert did: he sparked a stampede. The home-grown talent was left apologetically asking if it might dare to suggest that his analysis of the current situation was not perhaps slightly inclined towards the simplistic. What they should have said was that he was full of bull.

This is not to say that Mr Murdoch is stupid. He isn't: far from it. But he isn't *serious* about anything except business. The only thing he really knows anything about is newspapers, and he knows about those only to the extent that they are merchandise. He is a merchant. In many ways he is an impressive one, although he would be a more convincing multi-millionaire if he had not been born a multi-millionaire. Though I have never met him, I find him personally attractive, but that might be because I see him in the shaving mirror every morning. Rupert Murdoch is the man I might have been if I had been born rich, and thus felt obliged to spend my life proving that I was a self-made man. I would have had fun building empires, toppling governments, launching satellites to unleash Keith Chegwin on a helpless world. But by a stroke of luck I was given serious work to do.

Good television is serious work, even when – especially when – it looks most frivolous. Only someone with something to say can say something funny, unless you are the kind of person who laughs at nothing. I try to get the market price for what I do – the best guarantee of being able to go on doing it – but beyond that I don't make deals. I make things. Most people in British television take the same attitude. Rupert Murdoch, who makes deals, is talking a different language.

He is talking the American language. He always has. As with his newspapers, so with his television companies, he has spent his life matching the product to the market. In television he has seldom been successful even on his own terms. In Australia his Channel 10 was forever limping far behind Kerry Packer's Channel 9, which had senior executives who knew what they were doing. Murdoch always behaved as if it didn't much matter who ran the show as long as the right people owned it. The opposite, of course, is true: it doesn't much matter who owns the show as long as the right people run it. Even if Channel 10 had been a success, however, it would have been a success only within the framework of Australian commercial television, which is an American-style supermarket. The commercials come every few minutes at a level of noise that you can't turn down except by kicking in the set.

The real story of Australian TV is not of the commercial channels competing with each other to provide 'choice' (a word perpetually on Murdoch's lips), but of the commercial channels ganging up to compete against the ABC, which would be Australia's equivalent of the BBC except that it is chronically underfunded and has no prestige except with the educated public: the newspapers, nearly all owned by the same men who control the commercial television companies, vilify it on principle. It is important to remember that Rupert Murdoch grew up in an atmosphere where business ethics were the only ethics and public service broadcasting was despised out of conviction, with religious fervour.

Similarly, in the United States, Murdoch's Fox channel, which is fighting bravely to establish itself as a new network alongside NBC, ABC and CBS, can succeed, if it succeeds, only as part of the total failure of American television to provide a watchable service for people who can't stand being constantly shouted at to buy something. Once again, the real story is not of competition between commercial channels, but of their combination to stifle public service broadcasting. In the US, poor, embattled PBS is so starved of funds that a good proportion of its screen time has to be taken up by celebrities who have donated their charisma so as to help beg for money. Watching them panhandle is nearly as bad as being strafed by commercials.

For anyone who wants to avoid a serious brain operation, there can be no question of sitting down to watch American network TV for an evening. Those who praise the best products of American TV should be reminded of this fact, because if they omit it they are putting a sharp weapon in the hands of hustlers. The best American sitcoms *are* good. What's more, they are readily intelligible in Britain, whereas some of the best British products – *Auf Wiedersehen, Pet* for example – might as well be in German as far as the Americans are concerned. But the point to make is that the best place to *watch* American television is in Britain. If you love *Cheers*, don't watch it in America. It takes longer. There are commercials between the opening titles and the first scene. There are commercials between the last scene and the end roller. There are commercials between your heartbeats.

How did things *get* like that? Because business ethics were allowed to prevail over any other kind. Why is British television so much more civilised? Because American television was taken as a dreadful example. It should continue to be taken as a dreadful example. In Britain, television is central to the culture. In America it is inimical to the culture. American television can be exported in a relatively benign form because the countries who buy it, knowing what their markets will take, take only what they want. But the Americans themselves must take what they get. Their sovereign power of choice is exercised amongst infinite similarity.

If Britain wants a taste of how that feels, all it has to do is go ahead with the current proposal to auction off the commercial franchises to the highest bidders. The highest bidders will have the lowest foreheads. Worse, they will be clever people *pretending* to be stupid. It's already happening. When the ITV jingle for the autumn season came on the air, you heard a portent of the new age. 'Sahd bah sahd, get ready for ITV'. It was all done in an American accent. You can imagine the recording session. 'Sahd bah sahd' wailed the singers, going for another take: 'Get ready for ITV.' Silence. 'I thought that one sounded all right, didn't you, Julian?' 'Yes, Martin, but I still think they should pronounce it *Ah* TV. It makes no sense to say 'sahd bah sahd' and then say ITV.' 'They *have* to pronounce it ITV. People would think RTV was something else. Rotten TV or something. Sorry, love. Nothing we can do about it.' 'OK, everybody, it's a wrap.' And so we took another step towards the edge.

We don't have to go over it. All we have to do – and I don't hesitate to include myself in this, because even if I didn't feel that I belonged to British television, I would still feel that British television belonged to the world – is remind ourselves of what has been achieved. Murdoch has helped to remind us, by his sublime incomprehension. His masterpiece, the true expression of his creativity, Sky Television, is up there like an orbital garbage disposal grimly warning us of everything Britain can still manage to avoid – so long as it remains proud of what it's got.

Pride should never have faltered. That it did can be explained only through weariness. There is an analogy with the Weimar Republic, which, precisely because it was a functioning democracy, was attacked simultaneously from the Left and the Right so savagely that it gave up. Ever since, charges have been pressed against the victim. British television is likewise held to account for its own bruises. True, it is being kicked now only from the Right. But that's only because the Left's leg grew tired.

Twenty years ago, before I became a TV critic, left-wing commentators were employed practically full time in denigrating the broadcasting system. These weren't the mentally underprivileged types who came along later to make the Labour Party unelectable. These were the well-turned-out young intellectuals of the Free Communications Group, drawing salaries from the broadcasting system as they toiled to bring about its radical alteration, a burning necessity proclaimed by no less a panjandrum than Raymond Williams, who was taken to be an expert on mass communications despite, or because of, a style so turgid that he could barely communicate with his most abject worshippers.

Williams himself never let up on how the television channels were reinforcing the tyranny of a consumer society. Strangely enough, on the face of it, the BBC was somehow even more insidious at doing this than its commercial rival. He would go on BBC television in order to say these things. He droned on about the 'flow' of the television schedules, their allegedly remorseless hammering in the consumer ethic. For ten years, as a TV critic on this paper, I tried to do my share of pointing out that he was talking hooey, and that British television had a tremendous, unsummable variety. But the more you protested that the public showed every sign of being satisfied with what it was getting for the price of the licence fee, the more the left-wing intellectuals insisted that the public had been deluded. This last point was proved when the public unaccountably allowed Mrs Thatcher into 10 Downing Street, whereupon the left-wing intellectuals washed their hands of politics altogether, the proletariat having failed them.

Unfortunately, the television executives had been softened up by those long years of calumny. They had been called a mandarin caste for so long that they started to feel shy about it. Also they had grown so accustomed to fending off high-flown arguments that they had no armour against low-flown ones. The Free Communications Group had at least tossed in the odd mention of Gramsci. The Media Monitoring Group eschewed such frills. It just made outright accusations of treason. Nor did Norman Tebbit waste any time analysing the 'flow' of the schedules. He simply operated on the assumption that the BBC, because it wasn't controlled from Whitehall, was out of control altogether. It was historically unfortunate that the BBC, at that time, was short of top-echelon executives capable of telling Mr Tebbit to go jump in the lake.

Those in charge of the duopoly's commercial half, if not precisely glad to see the BBC sweating, were certainly not sad to escape censure. Then it was their turn to be caught flat-footed. The moguls wanted a piece of the action. The moguls and the Government were in cahoots. It wasn't fascism: nothing so intellectually challenging. It was just business. The television executives were paralysed by the shock of hearing their vocations questioned in such infantile terms. Nothing wears you out like arguing at an elementary level. A one-sided debate started, strident ignorance versus a pained silence. Filofax-minded Saatchi executives held the floor while people who had given their lives to public service broadcasting hung their heads. The discrepancy was already grotesque before Rupert Murdoch showed up in Edinburgh. We should thank him for demonstrating just how grotesque it was. The wolf had come to lecture Red Riding Hood on how to find her way through the forest.

Neighbours, one need hardly say, is not alone. All the world's best-loved soaps, and mercifully few of their pale imitators, are bought in by and screened on British television as it now is. They are there by public demand, so to that extent the contention that the public isn't being served is obviously wrong. The contention that the home-grown talent hasn't come up with anything except turn-of-the-century snobbery is obviously wrong too – a lie so big that it took away the breath of those who might have countered it, so that all they could stutter was *Brideshead Revisited, The Jewel in the Crown* and, after some thought, *Fortunes of War.*

There has always been, and if a workable system is allowed to go on working there will continue to be, a lot more than that: more, as I found in ten years of saturation viewing, than any single human being can take in. Ideally, the popular programmes have been well enough done to seduce the highbrow into wondering if popularity is something he ought to scorn, and the more demanding programmes made with a gift for lucid explanation that discourages the less-prepared viewers from believing that these things are not for them. And in between – the area where I myself like to operate – there has traditionally been the twilight zone where the eccentrics roam and rumble: Joseph Cooper and his silent piano, David Bellamy and his talking facial hair – weirdos, yes, but people, not specifically bioengineered television life-forms.

It took confidence to put all that together. If there has been a weakening, it has been because frightened executives have become too responsive to the accusation, levelled at them first from the Left and now from the Right, that they are élitists foisting on the public their unexamined notions of what is good for it. But they *are* the public. There isn't, or shouldn't be, a conflict. Good programmes are made out of belief, by people to whom it doesn't occur to doubt that they are part of the same community as the people watching. If that faith has been shaken, it needs to be restored.

G. K. Chesterton said of Dickens that the question never crossed his mind of writing what the people wanted: he wanted what the people wanted. He was not a snob. Rupert Murdoch would like it to be thought that he is not a snob either: but he is. When he self-righteously talks about giving people what they want, he is really talking about the commercial desirability of giving them what he, personally, doesn't want, and wouldn't have in the house: he is talking about the people as if they were a market, whose desires, however base, were some sort of moral imperative. But the Roman people wanted gladiators, and that didn't make it right. A large number of British people want the *News of the World*, but that doesn't make it good. Hardly anybody seems to want Sky Television, but that isn't what makes it bad. What makes it bad is that it has had scarcely any programmes worth watching. As Andrew Neil and his subordinates are now discovering the hard way, the idea, relentlessly propagated by both Left and Right, that the broadcasting system has been repressing a wealth of potential creativity, is moonshine. Talent is rare, and the talent to handle talent is rarer still. Only a certain number of people are capable of making a watchable television programme, and Mr Murdoch will not be able to acquire their services merely for money. People who want to make good television are working for much higher stakes than that.

They aren't, in short, just making merchandise. They are contributing to a culture. Proponents of deregulation like to soothe us by saying that culture will be taken care of for those who want it. But a living culture is much more than just some people watching ballets while everybody else watches game shows. It can't be catered for by niche-marketing. A living culture is the whole thing. British television covers everything that the country does. It brings the country together like nothing else. It gives, or should give, all the people something to share at a time when they are being otherwise encouraged to split up into separate income groups and fend for themselves, the well-off behind high walls and the losers outside shedding litter. This latter process is one the Saatchi brothers are understandably keen to encourage. Why waste time screening grand opera to people who can't afford Porsches? The last stage of fitting the product to the market is fitting the market to the product.

There are real criticisms to be made of British television as it now stands. It has been far too inclined to co-operate in the long, bloody massacre of the English language which already threatens to leave not a single grammatical English sentence alive. Czeslaw Milosz once said that the King James Bible must be preserved in use because it is the only thing believers and atheists have in common. Similarly, grammatical English – the only kind which can express meaning with full freedom – should be fostered by broadcasters, not frustrated. It is all right for the *EastEnders* to speak as they do as long as the linkmen don't join them. Luckily the linkmen are now speaking better again. One or two controllers have done what they should do: control. In other words, they have resumed the task of carrying the can; being responsible to the public as if they belonged to it; administering a valuable institution which, above capitalism as it is above socialism, helps to define and maintain a democracy.

Observer
15 October, 1989

Making Programmes the World Wants

(At the BBC's request, this speech was given at a dinner for the representatives of all the world's television services who had come to Brighton for the annual BBC Enterprises Showcase Week in March 1991. Since there was no way of dodging the problem posed by the multilingual audience, I tried to make a virtue out of embracing it. The cod-polyglot approach worked well enough for the message to register as an intentional change of pace, and I sat down congratulating myself on my global vision. The euphoria was dissipated later on when I was approached in the lobby by some delegates from the newly liberated East European countries who wanted to know what I had said. It turned out that they hadn't come to the dinner because they couldn't afford it.)

L ET ME first thank Will Wyatt* for interrupting his busy schedule to give me such a generous introduction. I'm grateful for his support because this short speech will be one of the most challenging performances I have ever tackled in my life. On New Year's Eve I was once again lucky enough to anchor the BBC programme which was seen in Britain, Australia and New Zealand: *The Review of the Year.* The audience was numbered in many millions, but at least they all spoke the one language. Here tonight there are at least thirty different languages. So I have to begin by saying Good Evening Ladies and Gentlemen. Welcome to Brighton. *Bienvenu en Bréton. Willkommen in Brichton. Bienvenuto in Brigitonia. Bienvenida en Brigatonades. Zdravtsvue, eto Brezhnevtograd. Vitam vas do Braitonu. Kore wa*

*Managing Director, BBC Television

Buraitonu desu. Dozo, ohairi nasai.

The effects of deregulation on the global television environment are extremely complex and in the last analysis utterly unpredictable. *Les effets de déregulation auf dem Umwelt televisivo globalmente considerato sind tellement taihen complicados und dans la ultima analisnost zenbu depourvu de la possibilità de se prevoir, sumimasen.*

But obviously I can't go on like this, and I've left out those of you who speak Dutch, Danish, Finnish, Portuguese, Swahili, Tamil, Urdu, Persian, Hebrew, Arabic, Mandarin, Cantonese and Australian with a Melbourne accent. You all speak more than enough English to understand me when you're here but although languages are my hobby I don't speak enough of them to understand you when you're at home. This fact drives me almost mad with frustration. I wish I could speak *all* those languages. I *like* the variety of the world's cultures. I'm sure even the many American delegates we have here tonight would be sorry if the English language came to dominate the world's airwaves as it dominates the world's airlines.

On the airlines there is a good case for having one *lingua franca* and one only, and English might as well be it. An airline pilot should have good eyesight, good digestion and good English. A few months ago I was flying into the very busy airport of Los Angeles after sunset and the captain invited me up to the flight-deck for the landing. I put on the head-set and I could hear the conversation between the control tower and all the planes waiting to land. It was dark, very dark. There was cloud. There were hundreds of planes and they couldn't see each other. I heard the man in the control tower saying, 'Air Guatemala 737, go from 3,000 to 2,000, cut your speed to 300, line up with the left runway, not the right runway, imperative you use the *left* runway, the right runway is occupied, please acknowledge.'

And I heard the Air Guatemala captain say, '*Che?*'

But in television we want variety, and of course we get it. As I've said, nearly all of you here speak excellent English but most of you when at home watch television in your own language, and why not? You're living in your own culture. And it's imperative that all those cultures be preserved in their full depth and richness. Every country has its resident experts who warn that imported television will destroy the national consciousness and replace it with *Dallas*, *The Waltons*, *Star Trek* and *Twin Peaks*. For more than forty years the world has been warned by wise and worried voices that American soap operas will destroy the planet. These wise and worried voices have recently changed their tune only to the extent of adding a further warning: that Australian soap operas are even more dangerous than American ones. Countries which survived the impact of J. R. Ewing in *Dallas* are told that Kylie Minogue in *Neighbours* will cretinise their children, unbalance their economy, wipe out the rain forest, and make a hole in the ozone layer. But really any country's culture can survive, and even benefit from, the impact of imported television, as long as the imports are chosen well and the national product is genuinely creative. And in a heartening number of cases that's exactly what it is.

In recent years I've flown at least three times a year to make programmes in the world's capital cities. We call these programmes *Postcards* and the idea is that I fly in not knowing very much and record my first impressions in the most truthful but attention-getting way possible. In Miami I fall off the water-skis, in Los Angeles I get fitted with a hairpiece, in Rome I spend all day trying to park my car, and in Tokyo I go to a Love Hotel and can't find the button to switch off the vibrating bed. In other words I play the innocent. In fact, of course, I have to prepare, and when I'm there I try to deepen the preparation by watching as much local television as I can.

And almost always I am drawn in, fascinated. Filming during the day I learn a lot, but alone at night in the hotel room eating a late room-service club sandwich by the light of the TV set, I learn more. When I filmed my *Postcard from Paris* I had to spend a whole day being driven around the Left Bank by that amazing woman, the novelist Françoise Sagan. Françoise Sagan is a writer of great intelligence but she has never learned how to make a car go slowly. Here in Britain they used to have a woman called Boadicea who drove like Françoise Sagan. Boadicea drove a chariot with swords sticking out of the hub caps. Her effect on pedestrians was less devastating than that of Françoise Sagan. Eventually Boadicea got her licence cancelled. This has never happened to Françoise Sagan. Instead, President Mitterrand keeps giving her medals.

After my day of dicing with death in Françoise Sagan's company I recovered at night by watching television. I was hugely impressed by the way the writers and intellectuals talked on programmes like *Apostrophe*. On French television, six intellectuals can all talk at once and you can still follow what they're saying. I like the general impression that they've all just come in from the café round the corner and that after the programme they'll go back to the café and continue the discussion. Back in Britain, I've been trying to get some of that same quality on my talk-shows for BBC 2. But it is very hard to beat the French at their own game. They have whole *brasseries* full of articulate high-brows who somehow know the secret of interrupting each other without getting angry. British intellectuals are fewer in number and on television tend to oscillate between being too polite to say anything or else sueing each other for libel. But I think we're getting somewhere, and I think the French have shown us how.

I've also learnt a lot from talk-shows in German. The best place to watch them is in a Swiss ski resort where you can tune into transmissions from Germany, Austria, and of course from Switzerland itself. Hearing half a dozen German-speaking historians discussing the Weimar Republic and the Third Reich was not only good for my rudimentary prowess in the German language, it also did wonders for my grasp of modern history. But the real revelation on German television was a show starring Willi the Hamster. It was a game show in which several couples competed for large prizes. The outcome was crucially influenced by whether Willi decided to jump down the hole, eat the cheese or just sit there breaking wind on a small scale.

Pardon, devo tradurre. Ein hamster, che s'apelle Willi-san,
dalla suo estomaco il vento poco poco pfft pfft kowashita imasu ne.
Capito? Verstehen Sie? Intende? Ponymaesh? Wakarimashita ka?
We brought Willi the Hamster's performance home
on video tape and incorporated it very successfully into
another show of ours called *Saturday Night Clive*, which is a
kind of round-up of all the world's craziest television. This
show transmits here and in Australia and New Zealand, as
well as through the BBC direct-feed to the Low Countries,
and to my great pleasure bootleg tapes of it were passed
around at student video parties in Prague during the Vel-
vet Revolution, but I have to admit that it has often been
condemned by our critics here as frivolous. When I was a
television critic myself, which I was for ten years, I would
have said that frivolity is important. You can find out a
lot about a country from what it considers frivolous. You
can find out a lot about affluent West German society by
watching Willi the Hamster in action. East German society,
which was the reverse of affluent, broke down the Berlin
Wall just to get at Willi. You find out that the Germans
are nearly as crazy about animals as the British. Also you
find out that the people of the *Bundesrepublik* have very
sensibly decided that a 7 series BMW may be perfect, but
it isn't everything. You can win one or lose one according
to whether Willi the Hamster goes down the hole, eats the
cheese, or breaks wind, and that's just how it should be.

I think the same applies to the talent shows on Italian
cable television. Filming in Rome, I watched them every
night. One man's talent consisted entirely of imitating farm-
yard animals very badly. The studio audience demanded
that he should stop doing it. Shows like that inspire Italian
intellectuals to predict the imminent collapse of civilisation,
but what impresses me is how everyone involved keeps
his dignity, and above all speaks so beautifully, even the
pretty girl who is dressed in not much more than feathers
and keeps the score. British feminists would say, no doubt
correctly, that she is being exploited, but all the British
feminists put together can't speak English as well as that
girl speaks Italian. She seems to be her own person and

having fun. In his wonderful film about *Fred and Ginger*, Fellini satirised a show like that, but you could tell he enjoyed it. A screen full of ordinary people who don't say 'um' and 'ah' – how do the Italians work the trick of staging an on-screen party you'd like to be at? If programmes like that are a cultural disaster, all I can say is that the Italians have a culture big enough, old enough and rich enough to afford a few disasters.

The same might be said of Japan. Through my own fault, I labour under a reputation in this country for being unkind about the sort of Japanese television game shows in which terrible things happen to the contestants. My scholarly interest in the subject started about seven years ago when I first saw a show called *Gaman*, which here we call *Endurance*. And certainly the contestants had a lot to endure. They hung upside down over a slow fire while their underwear was filled with cockroaches. They were zipped into sleeping-bags with live lobsters. The British audience rocked with delighted revulsion when they witnessed these things and my critics called me a racist.

But I had noticed that the contestants were all smiling. Clearly they felt less squeamish about cockroaches than the average British viewer. It was a different attitude to living things, and probably a healthier one. The show *was* crazy, but to say so wasn't necessarily to be disparaging of the Japanese. There are 125 million Japanese and quite a lot of them are perfectly capable of realising that the producer of a show like *Endurance* is out of his head, or, as they would say, *baka des', ne*. Meanwhile everyone concerned seemed to be having a wonderful time. Fascinated, I went to Japan and actually took part in one of those TV game shows, called *Takeshi's Castle*. It wasn't until I was in my tracksuit and crash helmet that I found out I was the only contestant older than twelve. I lost a paint-gun fight with a pack of children – I still think they cheated – and I ended up upside down in a pool of mud, but I had a ball. I learned a word: *Gambarimassho*! It means 'Hang in there'.

And in the hotel at night I watched television. I watched some of NHK's marvellous cultural programmes. I saw a programme on calligraphy that affected my entire outlook. Even though I couldn't understand what was said, I was riveted by the economical beauty of what was done. That's how I began, four years ago this week, to learn the Japanese language, of which, although I am a long way from mastery or even elementary competence, I have now acquired enough to say to our Japanese visitors that watching television in Japan was the beginning of one of the most thrilling aesthetic adventures of my life.

So when Britain, like America, sells programmes to other countries, it isn't selling just anything to just anybody. The idea that the rest of the world is virgin territory is one which I absolutely do not hold. Other countries are not virgins, and that's why they're worth knowing. Like love, the exchange of television programmes is something that best happens between consenting adults. The spread of the technology to new places, and the growth of deregulation in some of the old places, has made television global only in the sense that the total demand has swollen to exceed the possible supply. But that doesn't mean that there is a world market for junk. I once heard a British ex-foreign secretary, who had been invited on to the board of a video business, announce that he couldn't see how the business could fail, because there were so many people who wanted something that they were ready to pay for almost nothing. I wondered why Mrs Thatcher had ever accepted his resignation, because he thought exactly the way she did. They had both missed the point of British television. Its best programmes can be sold at a profit only because they are made with dedication.

The present government's assault on the British broadcasting system having by now been staved off* – principally because some of the younger ministers saw sense – it is perhaps now safe to point out the paradox which underlay that unholy crusade. British television was being told to be more profit-conscious by people economically too illiterate to realise what a profit-centre British television already was.

*Wishful thinking – C. J., 1992

Why are you all here? You're here because you know this is where the programmes are. Television is something Britain does so well that it's got something left over for everybody. Weight for weight, *per capita*, or by however these things are measured, Britain must be the world's most fruitful television culture.

The title could have belonged to America, of course. It would have done, if the American television system had been set up in the first place so as to favour Public Service Broadcasting. But it wasn't, and so the main American networks were artificially restricted to an audience of people who could bear to watch programmes interrupted by commercials every two minutes. On behalf of the smaller but self-selectingly more intelligent audience who want something better, the American PBS and cable companies – who probably wouldn't even exist if things had been more humanely organised in the first place – feel obliged to come here. They are very welcome, but let's be in no doubt why they, and all of you, come here to this market. It's because it's not just a market.

Television programmes are things of the spirit, items of expression. They are creations. Nobody knows how to make one out of *purely* commercial considerations. Somewhere along the line, people have to be hired who are working for more than just money. They are working out of belief. Great inventions like the David Attenborough nature series *The Trials of Life* are made by whole battalions of people who work out of belief, commitment, personal sacrifice and love. The idea that you can make television *only* in response to market forces is an idea that not even Rupert Murdoch can render plausible. In fact he can't really afford to hold it: not for long. Sky Television is up there, but there is almost nothing on it, and the sort of people who watch nothing don't buy anything, so the enterprise doesn't even make sense in commercial terms.

The British television system makes programmes you want because the programmes are made by people who want to make programmes. It's a tradition of pride in craft, of living for what you do, and not just for what you can get. The BBC is better because of the competition from ITV, but there can be no doubt that ITV would not take such a civilised form – the commercials so far apart, the companies so intent on turning out programmes better than they need to be – if ITV had not been obliged to parallel the BBC. Not yet, and I hope never, weakened by too many additional channels, the duopoly is at the heart of British television's success.

And at the heart of the duopoly is the BBC. Long ago, when television was still just an idea, the people charged with setting up broadcasting in Britain were a stuffy bunch who could have been taken for men of the Church if they had worn different collars. But they believed in serving the people, and so a decision was taken about broadcasting which has affected the lives of generations, and largely for the better. And I think it's not a coincidence, but a natural consequence, that creative people who feel that they are as one with the people as a whole – who don't look down on the viewer, but look at the world through the viewer's eyes – should make programmes that the world wants.

I am too aware of the magnificent achievements of British television as it has been, and as I hope it will go on being, to class myself as anything except a very low-ranking contributor to that total effort, but I would like to end by saying two things. First, under the BBC's exalted auspices, I have been honoured to give this speech and gratified by your attention. You have done me too much honour. *Une réve assouvi. Sono commosso. Wirklich fabelhaft. Do, itashimashita.*

And the second and last thing: I see from these print-outs that my *Postcard* programmes and talk-shows have been sold in Australia, New Zealand, Canada, Portugal, Germany, Finland, Spain, Belgium, Holland, the USA, Romania, Hong Kong, Norway, Yugoslavia, Japan, Bahrain and Quatar.

And what I want to know is: what happened to Austria, Bulgaria, Denmark, France, Greece, Hungary, Iceland, Ireland, Italy, Malaysia, Mexico, Korea, Pakistan, Sweden, Switzerland, Thailand, and the USSR?

Where are you? *Où êtes vous? Dove siate . . .*

Preaching to the Converted

(An after-dinner address to the BBC Board of Governors
and Management, Lucknam Park, May 1991)

H AVING MADE a career out of being a square peg in
a round hole, the wrong man in the right place, I
really shouldn't be too surprised that I am here tonight and
about to harangue an audience of highly qualified people on
the subject of their own business. Almost everyone here is
engaged from day to day in the administration of broadcasting. The most I ever do is broadcast, and although I have to
spend a long day in the office for every minute the show is
on the screen, most of the actual brain-work is done by my
string of estimable producers – more than three-quarters of
them women, but I don't complain about being dominated
– who understand the charts and the diagrams and actually
know how to arrange a satellite interview with Sylvester
Stallone's mother. Apparently it isn't enough to understand
the engineering, you have to book the right astrologer, who
might be unavailable because she's advising Nancy Reagan
on how to deal with Kitty Kelly without the strychnine
leaving any traces. It all takes a lot of phone calls.

And it all has to be cost-effective, and it all has
to happen. Talking about it is necessary but not
sufficient. The smartest move I ever made was to realise
how dumb I am at that stuff. So I got some help, and left
myself free to fizz with enthusiasm, confident that someone
else would steer me away from the cliff if I rode my unicycle
too fast with my mouth open and my eyes shut. I have
a great respect for the practical people in broadcasting.
That's you. My tribute to you this evening will be to try
not to say more than I know. As a consequence I will be
speaking very briefly.

Much of what I do know I learned as a critic, not because as a critic I learned a lot about how television works – a critic can't do that, and he makes a mistake if he thinks he can – but because as a critic I watched a lot. For ten years I watched more television than anyone else alive. There was a man in Florida who watched more than I did, but he ended up dead, when he accidentally ate the cardboard plate along with the reheated *chilli con carne*.

There were no reliable home VCRs for most of the period I was watching professionally. There was an unreliable one made by Philips that used to chew up the tape and spit it out like *fettucine*, but the Japanese had not yet arrived to save us. So I ran two TV sets at once and made notes from memory – a good aid to selectivity, incidentally. Most critics now don't quote effectively because they quote too much. The rewind button writes their column for them. But forget I said that.

Anyway, I saw a lot of TV and still do, and I think those who are concerned with it *should*, at every level, right to the top. They should live it and breathe it. The same applies to radio, and I apologise to those concerned with radio if I say little specifically on that subject tonight. I did a lot of radio when I was starting off, and I still love being on it as a guest, although radio is more demanding in some ways than television. Television doesn't mind dead air. You can stop and think for a while and look like Socrates. Try that on radio and they'll think you've passed out. But in the early days I wrote a lot of scripts for BBC radio and Philip French and my other producers helped to teach me the difference between easy-seeming eloquence and mere rambling on. The blue pencil was freely wielded, by people who knew a dangling participle when they saw one. Time was pressing and the test was relevance. Good training.

Radio continues to be the focal point of the BBC's effort to ensure that the language is used well. Tom Stoppard's latest contribution, I think, was in part his homage to that sense of dedication. The voice of the BBC travels furthest without a face, and there are places in the world where it is listened to in the sheltering dark by people who have no other food for their hope. Compared to radio, TV often strikes me as a more flamboyant but tongue-tied bigger sibling, all fluorescent-framed spectacles, unstructured shoulders, acrylic tie and misplaced emphasis. But it's the medium I know most about, although even as a critic I could never answer the most common question: 'What's the worst TV programme you ever saw?' they would ask.

'You mean which episode of *It's A Knockout*?' was my glib reply, but the fact was that I enjoyed *It's A Knockout*, especially when Eddie Waring was hosting the mini-marathon. I enjoyed *Ski Sunday* when David Vine was extolling the virtues of the athlete he called 'Britain's sole representative, Konrad Bartelski, the man with the Union Jack on his helmet.' Konrad isn't skiing for Britain these days but David is still up there on the mountain, and where once I found his expertise superfluous I now find his persistence inspiring. Television had all these human exotica. They were weird, but they were real. They had to be, because nobody could have made them up. I miss Barbara Woodhouse the way I miss my Aunt Dot, although the most my Aunt Dot ever did with a horse was to fall off it. Barbara Woodhouse could breathe up its nose. After that, the horse would do anything, and so would you.

I found almost everything instructive in some way. To find a TV programme I really hated, I had to wait until June 1989. I was filming in Shanghai, not Peking, but the quiet rebellion was happening in Shanghai too. For a few sweet days Shanghai Television broadcast the truth. I was watching when things got back to normal. Li Peng came on and spent a couple of hours or so denouncing the student leaders as counter-revolutionary terrorists. You didn't need a translator to get Li Peng's drift. That deadly voice of his droned on and on like a mandarin meat-grinder. On the Bund the previous night I had seen three hundred thousand people all keeping their silent, hopeful, doomed vigil, and most of them weren't even students. There were school teachers, factory workers, proprietors of chicken-claw soup take-aways, everyone except those suspiciously well-groomed party hierarchs like Li Peng. His one-man show was a truly awful television programme. Now, when people ask me what I think of Jeremy Beadle, I've got my answer ready. I know a TV station that's got a presenter who *really* gets on your nerves.

On the night Chinese television was plugged back into the mincing machine, I learned all over again that the one positive thing evil can do for us is to help define the good. If you want an example of TV that is absolutely regulated, Chinese TV is it.

Somewhere out at the opposite pole of human experience there is American television, which, despite all the evidence, we are still sometimes asked to admire – in fact some people now ask us to admire it more than ever, because, they say, it is increasing the range of choice. The American networks are indeed losing their combined share of the audience, and not before time. Cable and the other ancillary channels are making inroads. The whole American system is on its way towards the commercial ideal of niche marketing, where every programme is targeted at a specific audience who will buy the sponsor's or the advertiser's product. Nobody will see *Rigoletto* except people who will buy the Rolex. Serial killers will get their own serial. An infinity of channels, an infinity of choice, and the whole thing self-financing, with even a conciliatory smidgin of PBS so that the few remaining hopeless idealists can see the occasional series about the Civil War and be reminded what happened the *last* time anyone tried to secede from the Union.

I exaggerate, of course, but not by much: and only to sketch the position we might call absolute deregulation, when the free market holds sway. Such a system, or lack of it, has its merits, but the one thing it can't have is a common audience. With absolute deregulation, there is rarely a time when everyone watches the same programme and talks about it next day as a shared experience. With absolute regulation, the same applies, because the programmes are too boring, although I suppose Li Peng's speech was a kind of shared experience for the Chinese, pity help them.

Somewhere between absolute regulation and absolute deregulation is us: the British duopoly which, I think, offers, when it is working, just about as much choice as you can have while still retaining something most people can share. And my point is that this is a national achievement; one to be proud of; a *good* compromise which though difficult to justify in isolation is positively and precisely defined by what we know of the bad.

It can be said cynically that the BBC keeps ITV honest and ITV keeps the BBC human. Many things can be said cynically. But it should be said roundly, and more often, that the broadcasting system is an occasion for national pride, a creation – partly willed, partly accidental, perhaps modifiable, but certainly cherishable – possessed in common.

It should certainly have been said at the Edinburgh TV Festival in October 1989, when Rupert Murdoch made a speech characterising the British TV executives as an élite dictating to the public what they should watch – telling the people what is good for them instead of giving them what they want. The answer should have been that to impose your taste and to give people what they want are the same thing if you and the people are the same people. The answer should have been that the élite was all in Rupert Murdoch's mind. But the answer wasn't made: not that day, anyway, or not very loudly. Young Jaci Stephen of the *Evening Standard* asked Murdoch why he thought that being proprietor of the *News of the World* qualified him to talk about the health of the British media, but her lead wasn't followed up. There was a stunned silence from which the distant onlooker deduced that it had somehow got about that Mr Murdoch might have something apart from Mrs Thatcher's unqualified admiration; that there really was something called élitest establishment broadcasting; and that a brash piratical satellite alternative might be a corrective, a cure, or even a replacement.

Well, Mrs Thatcher has moved on, Sky Television

has absorbed BSB to prove that a shark's ability to swim isn't necessarily improved by swallowing a barrel of cement, and Mr Murdoch is in debt like Mexico. The broadcasting bill was tamed in its wilder proposals; even the government is acting older and wiser; and once again the great and the good, the back-room boys, the havers of a quiet word, the People We Know, all those shadowy well-connected manipulators who figure as villains in the vision of Kenneth Trodd, have had their way, as I think they should, when they are needed. I never knew how much I liked the old Establishment until Mrs Thatcher almost succeeded in exterminating it. Her egalitarian aspect always was the most frightening thing about her. It certainly frightened the Labour Party. Nothing ever scared Neil Kinnock more than the spectacle of that woman actually acting on his principles.

Still, the broadcasting institution has been protected, and especially the heart of it, the BBC. Or maybe that analogy is inexact, and in our broadcasting system the BBC is a giant bronze bell, of which commercial television is the clapper. But leaving that aside, I still wonder if the point was fully grasped about how close we came to a real crisis – the worst possible crisis, a crisis of confidence, an irreversible erosion of belief.

The crisis of the Church of England is that too many of its bishops, and some would say of its archbishops, don't quite realise that they are atheists, but have begun to suspect it. The BBC is an institution which would be in the same state of crisis if its administrators were to doubt their right to decide what should be made and broadcast. But there should be no question about that right, because it is a duty. Nor should there be any question about those in charge bowing to market forces, because they should already be listening to the public. How best to do so is always a question, but following the advice of hucksters is not the answer.

And in television, I am sure, the best way to maintain touch with the consumers is to be one. The really worrying aspect about the acquisition of responsibility is when it turns to power, and power turns away from the forum, into the cloister. We should be aware of that threat and beware of it. I am very conscious while I am sitting here that I am not watching television tonight. Thank God *Inspector Morse* isn't on. But *Sleepers* is, and I don't like missing that, either. Well done BBC for *Sleepers*, and well done ITV for *Inspector Morse*, and that's all the competition we need, I think. The talent pool can be spread only so far before it runs thin. Ten channels will give you ten car-chases, make no mistake.

One of the defences of properly scheduled network television intended for the whole family, as against a 50-channel remote control unit operated from a lonely bed full of crumbs, must be that a well-planned evening of television is a good night out you can spend in. I think that those involved in administering and making public service television should be suspicious of every week they spend in Edinburgh, every afternoon they spend at Ascot, every evening they spend in a conference centre like this one, and above all every holiday they spend stretched out on the deck of anybody's yacht. When the time comes for the renewal of the great charter, which I for one regard as nothing less than the Magna Carta of the modern intelligence, we must be able to defend the BBC with a whole heart.

Charges of non-profitability are easily warded off. I went to the BBC Enterprises Showcase in Brighton this year, and if that wasn't a profit centre I would like to know what is. Buyers were queueing up from all over the planet. BBC exports would be a profit centre for the country even if they only broke even. They bring the prestige that De Gaulle said was more valuable than anything; the prestige that is beyond the power of government; the prestige of the national spirit.

Even charges of élitism – whether levelled from the Right, or from the Left, should it ever rise again – can be warded off if the administrators are able to show that they are not a separate caste but the representatives of both the producers and the audience, doing their best for both sides, squaring the circle, living out the dilemma, the balancing act between the two separate forces neither of which is fully resolvable in terms of the other – the desire to entertain and the obligation to instruct.

But to lose confidence in the BBC's initial, and I think enduring, sense of mission would be to sell the past. That marvellous series about Charles Darwin sailing in search of knowledge was made out of *belief* – belief that those who didn't know should be told. The several marvellous series by David Attenborough about nature were made out of the belief, and the joy, that among those watching would be another generation who didn't know and should be told. One of those who didn't know, and was told, was my own elder daughter, who is now, partly as a consequence, studying zoology at university. Her life wouldn't be the same without the BBC. Nor would mine or anyone's here this week, or anyone's in ITV, or anyone's in the country. Institutions are valuable beyond governments and good governments realise it. Bad governments do too and pull the plug out of the wall, which I suppose by now is what some of you would like to do with me. But if any of my glib summaries have raised questions, I'll be glad to elaborate further if I can. If I can't, I hope the outbreak of a general discussion will enable me to submerge again after first thanking you for the honour of the invitation and the flattery of your attention.

On the Eve of Disaster

(An after-dinner address to The Royal Television Society,
Grosvenor House, May 1991)

W^E ARE gathered here tonight to extend our profound
fellow-feeling, understanding and sympathy to all
those unopposed incumbent franchise holders who bid
fifty million pounds when they could have bid fourpence.
Shareholders will be receiving a colour brochure explaining
what happened. A very thin brochure.

In the brochure it will be explained that there
was another bid but it didn't arrive in time. For
example, Border TV *was* going to be challenged by a
consortium from Paraguay headed by Martin Bormann
and Lord Lucan, with a very attractive ethnic strand
contributed by the participation of Pol Pot and Idi Amin
as advisers on minority groups. Government sources were
especially excited by this bid because of the commitment
from its treasurer, Ronald Biggs, to cut overheads by hitting excess cameramen from behind with a tyre iron. But
in the last-minute dash to get the bid in on time, Saddam
Hussein crashed the tank.

I fantasise, of course. All the contenders are serious
and most of them will pass the quality threshold; after
which the prize will go to the highest bidder, and *should* go
to the highest bidder, for having had a cool enough head
to figure out how simple it all was. All he had to do was
guess which programmes would attract an audience, guess
what they would cost to make, and subtract that amount
from his guess about how much advertising revenue there
would be if the government which first had this bright idea
continued on its inexorable path to economic triumph, and
then add something extra based on his guess about how

148

much higher a figure the other guys might guess if their guess was based on even less information than his. After that there was nothing left for an applicant to decide except whether to put the six-hundred-page application together with staples to prove he was cost-conscious or bind it in solid gold to prove he had adequate funds.

After *that* it was in the lap of the gods – or to put it another way, in the hands of the ITC, who from now until November will be weighing one application against another, which should be as good a method of deciding as any. In ancient Rome they used to slay an animal and examine its entrails. It was called the Franchise Round Haruspication and Cicero got very excited about it in his letters to Atticus. Classical scholars among you will probably remember the letter to Atticus in which Cicero complained that his consortium had bid too much for the Rome Breakfast TV Franchise against the incumbent, SPQR–AM.

Cicero wrote: 'I should never have gone in with Frostius and Bransonius. Those guys can blow a few billion sesterces and never feel the squeeze. But I, Cicero, have bet my toga.' They lost, of course. Mark Antony and Augustus kept the franchise, although they fell out subsequently over an Egyptian female presenter with a lot of eye make-up.

But for all the independent producers, and I know many of you are here tonight, there can be no doubt that the government's original determination to release a new wave of creative energy has been magnificently realised. The way things were, independent producers had to please a commissioning editor before they could get a programme on the air. Now they will have to please a commissioning editor who will have to please his programme controller who will have to please a central scheduler. A lot of creative energy is going to go into *that* process. There's going to be a whole new level of alertness and imagination in the independent production sector. Remember when you took your idea for a documentary feature on horse breeding in Berkshire to Channel 4 and found yourself pitching it to a commissioning editor who turned out to be an eighteen-year-old ex-song-plugger wearing an earring in his nose? Now you can rewrite your documentary as a drama series, call it *The Darling Studs of Bray*, and pitch it to the programme controller of the Parmalat Bosch Maxwell Berlusconi Consortium that takes over the combined South Eastern Flatlands franchise after the Pye, Sky and Ski Yoghurt Conglomerate sells out to Mitsubishi Maharishi. He promises you a prime-time slot if you agree to defer your fee until the second series because he can't afford to pay you for the first owing to the current restructuring of the finance package, the nice way of saying that his outfit still owns a piece of BSkyB and can't afford to let go because without the money that they *might* make from that they don't possess even the notional assets to borrow enough to service the debt on the money they borrowed to pay for the copying machine.

Having secured your agreement, the programme controller of Parmalat Bosch Maxwell Berlusconi Lorimar Loseley Acacia Honey & Stem Ginger Holdings – there's been another restructuring during the weekend – joins the long queue to see the central scheduler, after he's finished being fitted for his new Napoleon uniform, the one with the solid gold epaulettes. But the central scheduler doesn't schedule the first series of your series in prime-time on the network. It runs at 2 o'clock in the morning on Grampian after the sheep-dog trials retrospective with Gaelic subtitles for the deaf. Congratulations, you won't have all the nagging problems of making a second series. In addition, you have the privilege of finding out the real meaning of that pulse-quickening expression 'green field site'. A green field site is what you and your secretary are left sitting in after the bailiffs have taken away your filing cabinets. She can make you a cup of tea. They've allowed her to keep the mug, and you're it.

Let me be serious for a moment, and say that things could have been a whole lot worse. The quality threshold will probably be raised high enough to trip up the cowboys, unless their horses can jump. By a last-minute, desperately late rearguard action the responsible officials have been given a warrant to do their traditionally British thing, and act in the public interest. The government's original idea – by which I mean the *original* government's original idea, the Thatcher government's original, mischief-making, unfathomably ignorant idea – has been modified in the direction of civic responsibility. There are not many of its one-time proponents who now say that it has been diluted. On this topic there are very few free-market purists left. They are harder to find than communists in Budapest. But they were there once; and I think it remains important to point out what was wrong with the purist argument, which is that it was pure folly, and not just politically, but economically. The idea that Britain's broadcasting system – for all its drawbacks one of the country's greatest institutions – was bound to be improved by being subjected to the conditions of a free market: there was no difficulty in recognising that notion as politically illiterate. But for some reason people *did* have difficulty in realising that it was economically illiterate too. A television programme is not a commodity. It might become one, but it begins as a labour of love. In television, to make money you must first make things, and the things you make, unlike hardware, software or any other kind of ware, are things of the spirit. If the free play of market forces reaches the point where it subverts the free play of invention, there may be a brief flurry at the pig trough, but whatever happens next goes down the drain.

It was touching that one of Mrs Thatcher's supporters in her attitude to television was my compatriot Rupert Murdoch, who made an historic personal appearance in order to castigate the mandarins of the British television system for putting themselves above the people by dictating what they should be given, instead of giving them what they wanted. Leave aside for the moment the consideration that it is Mr Murdoch who is putting himself above the people by giving them, in his tabloid newspapers, what he wouldn't give his own children without a health warning. The salient point here was that a representative of Australian commercial television was in no position to lecture the representatives of the British television system about the free play of market forces, which have subsequently reduced the entire Australian commercial television structure to a smoking ruin.

The Australian equivalent of the BBC, the ABC, though as always criminally underfunded, is still being watched by a public grateful to get some refuge from what commercial television has become, which is something even worse than what it was. The money-making geniuses, the free marketeers, Mr Bond and Mr Skase and Mr Whoever-he-was, are broke, or dead, or seeing more of their families. Mr Grundy is still doing very well because Mr Grundy makes programmes about Australia that people in other parts of the world actively enjoy watching, a proposition he is able to test personally, since he lives in the Bahamas, where he doesn't have to watch Australian commercial television.

Those of you here tonight who represent incumbent franchise holders and who feel that you might perhaps have bid a little low against a plausible opponent, incidentally, might take comfort from the example set in Australia by Mr Kerry Packer. Mr Packer owned TCN Channel 9, the most profitable of the Australian TV companies and often admired for its sophistication, there being, to the quick eye, detectable slivers of actual programmes in between the commercial breaks. Mr Bond, an ex-Englishman hailed by the Australian press as a dinkum Aussie financial genius because of his flair for mounting a leveraged buy-out against the beer froth of rival brewers, offered Mr Packer a thousand million dollars for his TV station. Mr Packer, who had always operated on the assumption that there is one born every minute, but who had never before seen one the size of Mr Bond, said: 'Look, I love my TV station but if anyone else is going to own it, I think it should be you.'

Mr Bond then proceeded to demonstrate that a TV station, for a man with the right set of characteristics, is an unbeatable mechanism for accumulating debt, into which he sank at such a rate that Sotheby's in London had to lend him money with which to buy their pictures so that he could cover up the cracks on the walls of his lovely home. By that time the Australian press were not calling him a dinkum Aussie financial genius any longer. They were calling him a Pom. Mr Packer was able to buy back his beloved TV station for less than a hundred million dollars, putting him more than nine hundred million dollars ahead on the deal. The incumbent had come back.

Behind the almost instantaneous Australian disaster in television lies the more gradual American one. While American PBS remains equipped with little else but a begging bowl, the networks, which the almost unbroken commercial breaks have always rendered unwatchable to the intelligent viewer, have been steadily losing their audience to the cable channels. The resulting multiplicity of sameness is called 'choice' by free market theorists who have never spent a lonely evening with a remote control unit desperately searching in fifty different directions for a way through the swamp. Niche marketing has reached its apotheosis. Up-market consumers watching up-market programmes are reached by advertising for up-market products. Down-market consumers watching down-market programmes are reached by advertising for down-market products. Or you can opt out, at a price. To Mrs Thatcher's inner circle it sounded like a dream: just the way the National Health Service would be if it were run properly.

Bedazzled by elementary notions about the supposed benefits of deregulation in America, the Thatcher government's target was public service broadcasting. The BBC and ITV were thought of, correctly, as a single institution insufficiently responsible to 10 Downing Street. Mrs Thatcher thought the same way about the Houses of Parliament. When it was generally realised that she felt the same way about her own Cabinet, she was deposed. The current government is more civilised, but when the time comes it will try to rattle the BBC as ITV has been rattled. Nor is there any reason to believe that a Labour government would have any other attitude. I hope it will be remembered next time, as I think it was remembered this time – although it was a near-run thing – that the BBC and ITV may be rivals but each would be diminished without the other, and that a drain on the creative resources of either is a wound to both.

There is a Japanese parable about two friendly rivals, Mr Kobayashi and Mr Hashimoto. They are out walking in the forest when they suddenly come face to face with a snorting example of the dreaded high-speed giant wart-hog that eats human reproductive organs, the Nakahaka. The Nakahaka bares its two rows of teeth, flexes its over-developed hind quarters, and vibrates its stubby bristled tail, a sure sign that it is about to attack. Mr Kobayashi kneels down and starts putting on a pair of running shoes. Mr Hashimoto says 'Don't be a fool, Kobayashi. Nobody can outrun the Nakahaka.' Mr Kobayashi replies: 'I don't have to outrun the Nakahaka. I only have to outrun you.'

Those of you who have read *Made in Japan*, the excellent book by Mr Morita of Sony, will recognise that story, which he told with Japan and the USA in mind. Morita-*san* was trying to point out that the economies of the USA and Japan are bound together. In a similar way the two halves of the British broadcasting duopoly are bound together; in a fruitful way; and fruitful not just for the people who work in them. There are other nations where it is easier to get rich in television. But Britain is the place where television helps to enrich the nation. Television is one of Britain's best things; an institution, in a country whose institutions are its gifts to the world; and I know you all feel the same way, even at the height of the fuss, in the very flurry of the farce which has been imposed on us. But dignity has been maintained, as it always will be as long as the public is kept in mind and our own membership of it is not forgotten.

Chip, Chip, Chip

H ALF OF Britain's broadcasting system having been
put into turmoil by Mrs Thatcher, the newspapers
now seem bent on demoralising the other half. The tabloids, with a few posh papers grotesquely choosing to lend
them dignity, have lately been attacking the BBC in such
a concerted manner that you would think Fleet Street still
existed in the one place, with all its feature writers drinking
at the same pub. The attacks are mainly based on the hasty
interpretation of ratings, which are useful tools only if you
accept that they are not tea leaves. But the proprietors,
and below them the editors, want to hear a story about
the BBC in disarray.

So on every paper a journalist poises himself over
the tea cup, and in the course of time discovers, for
example, that although the huge audience watching the
BBC voices little dissatisfaction, this is only because the
people who *would* voice dissatisfaction are not watching,
and that the BBC is therefore no longer popular. Then he
calls up as many BBC bigwigs as he can get hold of, asks
them what they intend to do in the face of the imminent
collapse of their entire organisation, and notes down any
comment which sounds defensive. When the piece is published it sounds like the same piece in the other papers.
This is not surprising, since they all quote each other as
evidence, but it can be alluded to as a consensus when
a follow-up article is commissioned. 'A lot of people are
saying . . .' says the journalist on the phone, and if you
reply that the only people saying it are a lot of people like
him, he has secured from you a usefully defensive comment,
which scarcely needs to be misquoted. He will probably do
that anyway, but not necessarily out of malice. The chances
are that he couldn't get it right if he tried.

The journalist given the job of sniffing around the edges of the media is usually either some freshly hired young bright spark with terrific ambitions and no information, or else the office dunce completing a long career as the man chosen to pursue ambulances of secondary importance. If television is already at one remove from reality, then writing soft news about it must be at two removes at least. There is no point, however, in despising the scriveners. The proprietors are envious of television. Its partial deregulation is not enough for them, and not just because most of them would like to buy some of the fragments. They are simply envious of what they see as its power, and so give free rein to their editors, who are envious of what they see as its glamour. Since even the better tabloids largely live off a diet of television's leavings, there is humiliation to make the envy worse.

The *Daily Mail* got some of its own back last week when Lynda Lee-Potter, their sob-sister who knows the stars, took Terry Wogan on her knee while he complained, as well he might have done, that just because his show was coming off was no reason to treat him as a failure. The talk show for star guests on the plug circuit can have only a limited life and the *Wogan* version had remained a steady ratings-puller well beyond its allotted span, but none of the tabloids was interested in admitting that the BBC had got good value out of it. They preferred to use the word 'axed'. The *Mail* allowed Wogan to explain that he had not been 'axed' but forgot to add that it agreed with him. Later in the week it had another scoop, when the magician Paul Daniels turned up to file some complaints of his own. Without benefit of Lynda Lee-Potter, Daniels accused the BBC, in his own resounding words, of a whole string of crimes, the worst of which, as far as I could tell, was that the Television Centre security staff had failed to recognise him at the gate. There was also a lot of stuff about smut encroaching on family entertainment in prime time, but it was hard to avoid the impression that his idea of prime-time family entertainment placed heavy emphasis on card tricks, doves up the sleeve, and the mysterious bisection of a girl in spangles.

The *Mail* had a marvellous week at the BBC's expense and would probably have enjoyed itself just as much even if Viscount Rothermere had not already signalled his deep personal sympathy for deregulation by stumping up real cash instead of silly stories. He had a stake in New Era television and was in a consortium for one of the ITV franchise bids. The first project was a victim of the BSB débâcle and the second was a non-starter, but who knows what the future will hold?

Meanwhile to goad the BBC is a rewarding sport in itself. It makes a tabloid feel like a heavyweight. If the other tabloids get in on your story then a hazy notion may aspire to the status of a talking point, and all concerned can almost convince themselves that they are dealing with facts. Jonathan Powell, controller of BBC 1, replied to the Paul Daniels piece, which gave Peter McKay in the *Evening Standard* the chance to lard his uniquely somnolent column with the opinion that Powell would be wise to remain silent, and the further opinion that the BBC ought to be shrunk to a tenth of its present size. All the evidence suggests that Peter McKay writes his whole column on an intravenous drip, yet he must retain, if only barely, the strength to swallow, because a story which was already chewed to purée when it reached him he still managed to convert into a whiff of gas.

But I don't want to be cruel to Peter McKay. He is just a weather-vane. The truth is that the not very gifted feature writers and columnists who are always infringing on the regular TV critic's preserves would gladly do so from no other motivation but that television is easy to prate about. There is also the matter of the journalist's annoyance about the television person's supposed salary. The journalist imagines that his reader shares this annoyance, but in my experience the reader would do better to be annoyed about what the journalist is getting, and the journalist to be enraged at the proprietor. Journalists who write soft news about television work an easy day compared to the people they are disposed to pillory, and take little risk. Wogan is well paid but my own price for handling Oliver Reed or his equivalent three times a week would be ten million pounds for the first year, plus danger money.

My own fabulous BBC salary of £355,000 p.a. by the way, is just that – a fable. The figure was made up out of thin air by some woman at *Today* who later transferred herself to the *Independent*, where I hope they know which one she is and what she is capable of. I don't deny that I get the market price – it would be a foolish performer who took less, and no employer would negotiate with him again if he spilled the details – but it isn't mad money, and has to be worked for. No print journalist who has the peculiar abilities to do television is debarred from it by anything except his reluctance to engage in the long task of breaking in, creating the conditions in which he can continue to work, and taking the risk that anyone takes who sets out to make money by pleasing the public: that he might displease it. If he is unwilling to do that, he has no right to envy TV performers their take home pay. They are, after all, taking it to a home into whose front door the journalist cherishes the right to insert his foot. The journalist's proprietor, meanwhile, is exempt from speculation about *his* emolument, unless he is Robert Maxwell, who lumbered on without faltering until tiny Nisha Pillai of *Panorama* put a bolt into his shoulder, and he began to crash.

Maxwell was a minus billionaire, which ought logically to have made him one of the poorest men in history, but he paid himself well enough to gamble away in an hour at the tables more money than Wogan has made out of a selfless career of saving Hollywood film stars from the consequences of their own egos. There is a danger that Maxwell, because he borrowed money and then stole it, will make Rupert Murdoch, who merely borrowed it, look public-spirited. And indeed Murdoch, though at one time an even more poverty-stricken minus billionaire than Maxwell ever was, is a man of principle; but I doubt if anyone British-born, even his friend Mrs Thatcher, really appreciates what his principles are. For instance, he regards the very idea of public service broadcasting as an offence. Mrs Thatcher would have been prepared to live with the broadcasting system after what she thought of as the clear wind of market forces had been allowed to blow through it. Mr Murdoch dreams of that same wind blowing it away. He believes that Britain will be a better place when Sky attains break-even point, which will apparently happen when a big enough proportion of homes have been 'penetrated' – a polite way of saying shafted.

Sky will probably make it. First of all it has developed and successfully applied its own wonderful special branch of the accountant's language, by which if the weekly loss is halved it becomes a profit, even if it is still in millions. Second, the man in charge is Sam Chisholm, one of Murdoch's true assets. If the banks ever decided that Murdoch's total burden of debt had shrunk to the extent that they might risk closing him down, Chisholm would be one of the components worth bidding for. In Australia he used to head up Channel 9 for Kerry Packer, one of Australia's few plus billionaires. Chisholm ran Packer's channel as a bright, loud supermarket which perennially out-shouted Murdoch's Channel 10. Murdoch's channel never matched Packer's except in the year that Murdoch bought the Olympics. (If it turns out in the near future that you can't watch Wimbledon on the BBC, that will be the signal that Sky is making its big push for final penetration.) Chisholm has an appetite for efficiency so mighty that he has even been able to digest the awkwardly shaped, sharp-cornered fixed assets of BSB. He also has the advantage of being backed by Sky's great weapon, the Murdoch press.

The Murdoch tabloids, while never ceasing to fill their pages with stories in which real life and television soap operas are inextricably confused, hammer away at the BBC with all the envy of their rivals plus a more virulent element: self-righteousness. Suddenly every think-piece writer and philosopher on the *Sun*, the *News of the World* and *Today* becomes an expert on ratings and a tribune of the people's rights. Disgracefully, the *Sunday Times* has joined in the campaign. Andrew Neil, its editor, would probably resent the implication that he is a creature of Murdoch's will. He would like to think that he has a mind of his own. But the pilot-fish, though it might feel that it is leading the shark, is just riding in its pressure wave. In the issue before last the *Sunday Times* carried a story about the BBC's ratings which Andrew Neil would probably not have published if it had not suited his prejudices, and if his prejudices, alas, had not suited Murdoch's. It took two reporters to write the piece, with 'additional reporting' by a third. Ranking mercifully low among those quoted, I was cold-called by the third, who politely listened to the same line of argument which you are reading now. I also said, in passing, that I thought there was an industry-wide lack of sitcom writing talent, mainly because of the distorting influence of Hollywood. This was the bit that got into the article, but by the time it did the industry-wide deficiency had become the BBC's deficiency. I found myself attacking the BBC, in quotation marks. After years of making speeches defending Britain's classic broadcasting system from ideologues and hucksters, I had managed to enlist myself among its attackers.

Let me strongly advise my fellow talking heads against falling into the same trap. Watch out for the third man, the one doing the additional reporting. If he doesn't misquote what you said, the other two will scramble what he said you said, and somehow your voice will join the consensus.

There are criticisms to be made of the BBC, but the critic must first wipe his nose free of wet tea leaves. BBC 1 and BBC 2 badly need a combined strategy. There was a time when formats could be tried and tested on BBC 2 before they were switched to BBC 1 to take the heat. That strategy, or something like it, needs to be re-established, and made mandatory. The matter might almost be described as urgent, if the tabloids weren't waiting to pounce.

It could be said – Paul Johnson *has* said it, in this paper – that Britain's classic broadcasting system is defended by those who stand to gain from it. They do, but not necessarily in cash. ITV pays better than the BBC, and deregulated television pays better than anyone. In America Dan Rather's price goes up as his network's audience-share goes down, because the size of the audience he does pull comes to matter more. Sam Chisholm of Sky, with Keith Chegwin at his disposal, will probably never call me up, but if he does then I am sure the salary he mentions will be dazzling. What I am after, though, is the audience: the whole audience, or as much of it as I can pull into the tent. That might sound like arrogance but there is a sly modesty which is more arrogant still.

Rupert Murdoch despises the mandarins who presume to decide what the people ought to have. He thinks there is a clear distinction between that and giving the people what they want. But you don't have to be a mandarin to be confident about giving the people what you think they ought to have. All you have to be is one of the people. The deregulators who want nothing but niche marketing call it democracy. If it is, it is a mean conception of it. It has been said that satellite and cable channels don't broadcast, they re-broadcast. This is far closer to the truth than anything their champions say about the classic system. The first series of the BBC serial *The House of Eliott* was not only not the ratings failure some of the papers called it, it was more than a ratings success. It pulled a huge family audience while the satellite and cable channels were screening stuff a decade old, and even ITV was showing a movie.

The BBC as it has always been, and ITV as we hope it will be again once it gets itself back together, constitute a productive force which is beyond markets, and can be assessed only as part of a culture – perhaps even the most important part, because although we can't be sure that values are transmitted by a good book, we are somehow certain they are traduced by a bad programme. Of the duopoly's two components, the BBC is currently the more vulnerable. Until its charter is renewed, it must plead to be appreciated by the least fair-minded yet most influential minority in its audience – parliamentarians without time to watch it and press executives who would like to see it whipped. At the rate the press is going, the question will become not whether the BBC needs to be broken up, but how. This growing capacity of Britain to attack its own institutions is beginning to look suicidal.

They are, after all, the reason why some of us came here. Rupert Murdoch is here on his way to America, the centre of his world, which is commercial pure and simple. But there are those among his fellow expatriates who are here for what Sir Winston Churchill, when he saw it threatened, called the life of Britain, her message and her glory. Your broadcasting system is part of what holds you together. Pull it to pieces and you tear at your own heart. Having lived here for thirty years I can't plausibly invoke the visitor's privilege of saying that I hate to see you doing this to yourselves, so all I can do is just feebly wish that the tripe might be confined to the comic papers. Serious ones, including Murdoch's if their editors are brave enough, should cut out the nonsense.

Spectator
14 December, 1991

Part Three:

RECENT VERSE

Jet-lag in Tokyo

Flat feet kept Einstein out of the army.
The Emperor's horse considers its position.
In Akasaka men sit down and weep
Because the night must end.

At Chez Oz I discussed my old friend's sex change
With a lovely woman who, I later learned,
Had also had one. The second movement
Of the Mahler Seventh on my Boodo Kahn
Above the North Pole spoke to me like you.

Neutrinos from 1987A
Arrived in the Kamikande bubble-chamber
Three hours before the light. Shinjuku neon
Is dusted with submicroscopic diamonds.

Our belled cat keeps blackbirds up to scratch
With the fierce face of a tiger from the wall
Of the Ko-hojo in the Nanzen-ji, Kyoto.
You would not have been looking for me,
God told Pascal,
If you had not found me.

What will we do with those Satsuma pots
When the sun dies? Our Meissen *vieux Saxe* girl
Was fired three times. The car will be OK:
A Volkswagen can take anything.

An age now since I wrote about your beauty,
How rare it is. Tonight I am reminded.
Sue-Ellen Ewing says *Gomen nasai.*
Perhaps the Emperor's horse is awake also.
I think this time I've gone too far too fast.

The Light Well

Nacimos en un país libre que nos legaron nuestros padres, y primero se hundirá la Isla en el mar antes que consintamos en ser esclavos de nadie.

Fidel Castro, *La historia me absolverá*

From Playa de Giron the two-lane blacktop
Sticks to the shoreline of the Bay of Pigs –
The swamp's fringe on your left showing the sea
Through twisted trees, the main swamp on your right –
Until the rocks and tangled roots give way
To the soft white sand of Playa Larga,
The other beach of the invasion. Here
Their armour got stopped early. At Giron
They pushed their bridgehead inland a few miles
And held out for two days. From the air
Their old B-26s fell in flames.
High-profile Shermans doddered, sat like ducks
And were duly dealt with. Fidel's tanks,
Fresh in from Russia and as fast as cars,
Dismembered everything the Contras had,
Even the ships that might have got them out.
Also the People, who were meant to rise –
Chuffed at the thought of being once again
Free to cut cane all day for one peso
On land owned by the United Fruit Company –
Unaccountably stayed where they were. The swamp
Didn't notice a thing. The crocodiles
Haven't given it a thought in years,
Though wayward bombs from 4.2" mortars

166

Must, at the time, have made some awfully big
Holes in the mud. Apart from the vexed question
Of which genius ever picked it as the venue
For a military initiative whose chance
Paled beside that of a snowball in Hell,
The area holds no mysteries. Except one.
Somewhere about a mile along the road,
Look to the right and you can see a hint
Of what might be a flat spot in the swamp.
It is. A sketchy dirt track through the trees
Leads to a pool just forty feet across
Connected to the sea at such a depth
That though as clear as air and always calm
It shades down into darkness. Sufferers
From vertigo can't swim there. Parrot fish
Like clockwork paperweights on crystal shelves,
Their colour schemes preposterous, exchange
Positions endlessly. Shadows below
Look no more dense than purity compressed
Or light packed tight. Things were clear-cut
At that great moment of assault repulsed,
The victors proud yet chivalrous to a fault.
White flags, no matter how unsavoury
The hands that held them, were respected. Two
Of Batista's most notorious torturers,
Still wearing their original dark glasses
(Through which they'd both looked forward to a prompt
Resumption of a glittering career),
Were singled out and shot, but otherwise
Nobody missed a change of socks. They all
Got shipped back undamaged to Miami –
A better deal than they'd have handed out.
That day the Cuban revolution showed
A cleanliness which in the memory
Dazzles the more for how it has been spoiled:
What had to happen sullied by what might
Have been avoided, had those flagrant beards
Belonged to wiser heads – or so we think,
We who were young and thrilled and now are neither.

Credit where credit's due, though. Let's be fair.
Children cut cane here still, but go to school,
And don't get sick; or, if they do, don't die.
La cienega is a charnel house no longer,
And in this pool, which they call El Senote,
Young workers float at lunchtime like tree frogs
Poised on an air column. Things have improved
In some ways, so when they get worse in others
It's easier to blame Reagan than accept
The plain fact that the concentrated power
Which makes sick babies well must break grown men –
The logic so obvious it's blinding.
From armchairs far away we watch the brilliant
Picture grow dim with pain. On the Isle of Pines
The men who wear dark glasses late at night
Are back in business. Anyone smart enough
To build a raft from inner tubes and rope
Would rather run the gauntlet of the sharks
On the off-chance of encountering Florida
Than take the risk of listening to one more
Speech by Fidel – who, in his unrelenting
Urge to find friends among the non-aligned
Countries, now heaps praise on the regime
Of the Ayatollah Khomeini. Russian oil
Pollutes Havana. How opaque, we feel,
Those erstwhile glories have become, how sad –
Preferring, on the whole, to leave it there
Than enter beyond one long, ravished glance
That cistern filled with nothing but the truth,
Which we partake of but may not possess
Unless we go too deep and become lost,
By pressure of transparency confounded –
Trusting our eyes instead of turning back,
Drawn down by clarity into the dark,
Crushed by the prospect of enlightenment,
Our lungs bursting like a revelation.

Bring me the sweat of
Gabriela Sabatini

Bring me the sweat of Gabriela Sabatini
For I know it tastes as pure as Malvern water,
Though laced with bright bubbles like the aqua
   minerale
That melted the kidney stones of Michelangelo
As sunlight the snow in spring.

Bring me the sweat of Gabriela Sabatini
In a green Lycergus cup with a sprig of mint,
But add no sugar –
The bitterness is what I want.
If I craved sweetness I would be asking you to bring me
The tears of Annabel Croft.

I never asked for the wrist-bands of Maria Bueno,
Though their periodic transit of her glowing forehead
Was like watching a bear's tongue lap nectar.
I never asked for the blouse of Françoise Durr,
Who refused point-blank to improve her soufflé serve
For fear of overdeveloping her upper arm –
Which indeed remained delicate as a fawn's femur,
As a fern's frond under which cool shadows gather
So that the dew lingers.

Bring me the sweat of Gabriela Sabatini
And give me credit for having never before now
Cried out with longing.
Though for all the years since TV acquired colour
To watch Wimbledon for even a single day
Has left me shaking with grief like an ex-smoker
Locked overnight in a cigar factory,

Not once have I let loose as now I do
The parched howl of deprivation,
The croak of need.

Did I ever demand, as I might well have done,
The socks of Tracy Austin?
Did you ever hear me call for the cast-off Pumas
Of Hana Mandlikova?
Think what might have been distilled from these things,
And what a small request it would have seemed –
It would not, after all, have been like asking
For something so intimate as to arouse suspicion
Of mental derangement.
I would not have been calling for Carling Bassett's
    knickers
Or the tingling, Teddy Tinling B-cup brassière
Of Andrea Temesvari.

Yet I denied myself.
I have denied myself too long.
If I had been Pat Cash at that great moment
Of triumph, I would have handed back the trophy
Saying take that thing away
And don't let me see it again until
It spills what makes this lawn burst into flower:
Bring me the sweat of Gabriela Sabatini.

In the beginning there was Gorgeous Gussie Moran
And even when there was just her it was tough enough,
But by now the top hundred boasts at least a dozen
    knock-outs
Who make it difficult to keep one's tongue
From lolling like a broken roller blind.
Out of deference to Billie-Jean I did my best
To control my male chauvinist urges –
An objectivity made easier to achieve
When Betty Stove came clumping out to play
On a pair of what appeared to be bionic legs
Borrowed from Six Million Dollar Man.

I won't go so far as to say I harbour
Similar reservations about Steffi Graf –
I merely note that her thigh muscles when tense
Look interchangeable with those of Boris Becker –
Yet all are agreed that there can be no doubt
About Martina Navratilova:
Since she lent her body to Charles Atlas
The definition of the veins on her right forearm
Looks like the Mississippi river system
Photographed from a satellite,
And though she may unleash a charming smile
When crouching to dance at the ball with Ivan Lendl,
I have always found to admire her yet remain detached
Has been no problem.

But when the rain stops long enough for the true beauties
To come out swinging under the outshone sun,
The spectacle is hard for a man to take,
And in the case of this supernally graceful dish –
Likened to a panther by slavering sports reporters
Who pitiably fail to realise that any panther
With a top-spin forehand line drive like hers
Would be managed personally by Mark McCormack –
I'm obliged to admit defeat.

So let me drink deep from the bitter cup.
Take it to her between any two points of a tie-break
That she may shake above it her thick black hair,
A nocturne from which the droplets as they fall
Flash like shooting stars –
And as their lustre becomes liqueur
Let the full calyx be repeatedly carried to me.
Until I tell you to stop
Bring me the sweat of Gabriela Sabatini.

Drama in the Soviet Union

When Kaganovich, brother-in-law of Stalin,
Left the performance barely halfway through,
Meyerhold must have known that he was doomed,
Yet ran behind the car until he fell.
In *Pravda* he'd been several times condemned
For Stubborn Formalism. The ill will
Of the All Highest himself was common knowledge,
Proved by a mud-slide of denunciations
And rubbed in by the fact that the Great Teacher
Had never personally entered the theatre
Which this enemy of the people had polluted
With attitudes hostile to the State.

Thus Meyerhold was a dead man of long standing:
Behind the big black car it was a corpse
That ran, a skull that gasped for air,
Bare bone that flailed and then collapsed.
His dear friend Shostakovich later said
How glad he was that he had never seen
Poor Meyerhold like that. Which was perhaps
Precisely why this giant of his art
Did such a thing: to dramatise the fear
Which had already eaten him alive
And make it live.

       Stalin, meanwhile,
Who didn't need to see how it was done
To know that the director's trick of staging
A scene so it could never be forgotten
Had to be stamped on, was the acknowledged master
Of the one theatrical effect that mattered –
He knew how to make people disappear.

172

So Meyerhold, having limped home, plummeted
Straight through the trap-door to oblivion.
Nobody even registered surprise.
Specific memories were not permitted.
People looked vague, as if they didn't have them.
In due course his widow, too, was murdered –
Stabbed in the eyes, allegedly by thieves.

Go back to the opal sunset

Go back to the opal sunset, where the wine
Costs peanuts, and the avocado mousse
Is thick and strong as cream from a jade cow.
Before the passionfruit shrinks on the vine
Go back to where the heat turns your limbs loose.
You've worked your heart out and need no excuse.
Knock out your too-tall tent-pegs and go now.

It's England, April, and it's pissing down,
So realise your assets and go back
To the opal sunset. Even Autumn there
Will swathe you in a raw-silk dressing-gown,
And through the midnight harbour lacquered black
The city lights strike like a heart attack
While eucalyptus soothes the injured air.

Now London's notion of a petty crime
Is simple murder or straightforward rape
And Oxford Street's a bombing range, to go
Back to the opal sunset while there's time
Seems only common sense. Make your escape
To where the prawns assume a size and shape
Less like a new-born baby's little toe.

Your tender nose anointed with zinc cream,
A sight for sore eyes will be brought to you.
Bottoms bisected by a piece of string
Will wobble through the heat-haze like a dream
That summer afternoon you go back to
The opal sunset, and it's all as true
As sand-fly bite or jelly-blubber sting.

What keeps you here? Is it too late to tell?
It might be something you can't now define,
Your nature altered as if by the moon.
Yet out there at this moment, through the swell,
The hydrofoil draws its triumphant line.
Such powers of decision should be mine.
Go back to the opal sunset. Do it soon.

Budge up

Flowering cherry pales to brush-stroke pink at blossom fall
Like watermelon bitten almost to the rind.
It is in his mind because the skin is just that colour
Hot on her tight behind
As she lies in the bath, a Bonnard flipped like a flapjack.

His big black towel turns a naiad to a dryad,
Then, no pun intended.
An unwrapped praline,
She anoints herself with liberal Oil of Ulay.
It looks like fun.
Her curved fingers leave a few streaks not rubbed in.
He says: here, let me help.

The night is young but not as young as she is
And he is older than the hills.
Sweet sin
Swallows him at a gulp.

While cherry blossom suds dry on the lawn
Like raspberry soda
He attends the opening of the blue tulip
Mobbed at the stage door by forget-me-nots.

For a short season
He basks in her reflected glory.

Pathetic fallacy,
Dispelled by the clattering plastic rake.

The Artificial Horizon

Deus gubernat navem

The artificial horizon is no false dawn
But a tool to locate you in the sky.
A line has been drawn.
If it tilts, it is you that are awry.
Trust it and not your eye.

Or trust your eye, but no further than it goes
To the artificial horizon.
Only if that froze
Would you look out for something on the level
And pray you didn't spot it too late.
To stay straight
You can't just follow your nose –

Except when the true horizon's there.
But how often is that?
The sea at sunset shades into the air.
A white cloud, a night black as your hat –
What ground you glimpse might be at an angle,
While looking flat.

So the artificial horizon is a court
Of appeal, your first line of defence
And last resort:
A token world whose import is immense.

Though it seem unreal,
If it moves it can't be broken.
Believe that it makes sense
Or else be brought up short.

The artificial horizon
Is your Dr Johnson:
It's got its own slant.

It says clear your mind of cant.

Last night the sea dreamed it was Greta Scacchi

Last night the sea dreamed it was Greta Scacchi.
It wakes unruffled, lustrous, feeling sweet –
Not one breath of scandal has ever touched it.

At a higher level, the rain has too much power.
Grim clouds conspire to bring about its downfall.
The squeeze is on, there is bound to be a shake-out.

The smug sea and the sky that will soon go bust
Look like antagonists, but don't be fooled:
They understand each other very well.

We are caught between the hammer and the anvil.
Our bodies, being umpteen per cent water,
Are in this thing up to the neck at least.

If you want to feel detached from a panorama,
Try the Sahara. Forget about Ayers Rock –
The sea was once all over it like a rash.

The water in the opal makes it lovely,
Also unlucky. If not born in October
You might be wearing a cloudburst for a pendant.

The ban on flash photography is lifted.
The reception area expectantly lights up.
No contest. It's just life. Don't try to fight it –

You'll only get wet through, and we are that
Already. Every dimple in the swell
Is a drop in the ocean, but then who isn't?

No, nothing about women is more sensual
Than their sea smell. Look at her lying there,
Taking what comes and spreading it on her skin –

The cat, she's using her cream as moisturiser.
Milt Jackson's mallets bounce on silver leaves.
Strafed by cool riffs she melts in silent music:

Once we walked out on her, but we'll be back.

What Happened to Auden

His stunning first lines burst out of the page
Like a man thrown through a windscreen. His flat drawl
Was acrid with the spirit of the age –
The spy's last cigarette, the hungry sprawl
Of Hornby clockwork train-sets in 'O' gauge,
Huge whitewashed slogans on a factory wall –
It was as if a spotlight when he spoke
Brilliantly pierced the histrionic smoke.

Unsentimental as the secret police,
Contemporary as a Dinky Toy,
On holiday in Iceland with MacNeice,
A flop-haired Cecil Beaton golden boy,
Auden pronounced like Pericles to Greece
The short time Europe had left to enjoy,
Yet made it sound as if impending doom
Could only ventilate the drawing-room.

Splendidly poised above the ashtray's rim,
The silver record-breaking aeroplane
For streamlined utterance could not match him.
Oblique but no more often than the rain,
Impenetrable only to the dim,
Neurotic merely not to be insane,
He seemed to make so much sense all at once
Anyone puzzled called himself a dunce.

Cricket pavilion lust looked a touch twee
Even to devotees, but on the whole,
Apart from harsh reviews in *Scrutiny*,
All hailed his triumph in Cassandra's role,
Liking the *chic* he gave her, as if she

Wore ankle-strap high heels and a mink stole –
His ambiguity just further proof
Here was a man too proud to stand aloof.

By now, of course, we know he was in fact
As queer as a square grape, a roaring queen
Himself believing the forbidden act
Of love he made a meal of was obscene.
He could be crass and generally lacked tact.
He had no truck with personal hygiene.
The roughest trade would seldom stay to sleep.
In soiled sheets he was left alone to weep.

From the Kurfürstendamm to far Shanghai
He cruised in every sense with Isherwood.
Sadly he gave the talent the glad eye
And got out while the going was still good.
New York is where his genius went to die
Say those who disapproved, but though they could
Be right that he lost much of his allure,
Whether this meant decline is not so sure.

Compatriots who stuck it out have said
Guilt for his getaway left him unmanned,
Whereat his tap-root shrivelled and went dead,
Having lost contact with its native land.
Some say it was the sharing of his bed
With the one man nobody else could stand
That did him in, since poets can't afford
The deadly risk of conjugal concord.

But Chester made bliss hard enough to take,
And Wystan, far from pining for his roots,
Gaily tucked into the unrationed steak.
An international figure put out shoots.
Stravinsky helped the progress of the rake:
Two cultural nabobs were in cahoots.
No, Auden ageing was as much at home
On the world stage as Virgil was in Rome,

If less than *salonfähig* still. Regret
By all accounts he sparingly displayed
When kind acquaintances appeared upset,
Their guest-rooms wrecked as if by an air-raid.
He would forgive himself and soon forget.
Pig-like he revelled in the mess he made,
Indecorous the more his work lost force,
Devoid of shame. Devoured, though, by remorse,

For had he not gazed into the abyss
And found, as Nietzsche warned, that it gazed back?
His wizardry was puerile next to this.
No spark of glamour touched the railway track
That took whole populations to the hiss
Of cyanide and stoked the chimney stack
Scattering ash above a vast expanse
Of industry bereft of all romance.

The pit cooled down but still he stood aghast
At how far he had failed to state the case
With all those tricks that now seemed so half-arsed.
The inconceivable had taken place.
Waking to find his wildest dreams outclassed
He felt his tongue must share in the disgrace,
And henceforth be confined, in recompense,
To no fine phrase devoid of plain prose sense.

The bard unstrung his lyre to change his tune,
Constrained his inspiration to repent.
Dry as the wind abrading a sand dune,
A tightly drafted letter of intent,
Each rubric grew incisive like a rune,
Merest suggestions became fully meant.
The ring of truth was in the level tone
He forged to fit hard facts and praise limestone.

His later manner leaves your neck-hair flat,
Not standing up as Housman said it should
When poetry has been achieved. For that

In old age Auden simply grew too good.
A mortal fear of talking through his hat,
A moral mission to be understood
Precisely, made him extirpate the thrill
Which, being in his gift, was his to kill.

He wound up as a poor old fag at bay,
Beleaguered in the end as at the start
By dons appalled that he could talk all day
And not draw breath although pissed as a fart,
But deep down he had grown great, in a way
Seen seldom in the history of his art –
Whose earthly limits Auden helped define
By realising he was not divine.

Part Four:

WHIPPING THEM IN

Incredible Two-headed Man

WHEN MY executive producer Richard Drewett and I transferred from ITV to the BBC in 1990, we took with us the exiguous footage of a prospective documentary we had shot on spec when I had hosted the Frank Sinatra concert that opened a luxury resort called Sanctuary Cove, near Surfers' Paradise in Queensland. While our office was being set up at BBC Kensington House we camped in the editing rooms and painstakingly assembled 'Clive James Finally Meets Frank Sinatra'. Short of options, we had to print shots twice and run some of them backwards. I wrote at least ten complete drafts of the commentary with strips of film hanging around me like drying kelp. Struggling to get the thing finished by the scheduled screening date, we were unsettled to discover that the news had been announced, and in a dangerously misleading form. The word was out that we had a full length, fifty-minute interview with Sinatra. Actually we had more like five minutes, which, although it was four minutes more than he had given anyone for years, was going to look pretty feeble unless something could be done to pre-empt the press. So I took up the *Observer Magazine* on its generous long-standing offer to print any feature I felt like. Without exactly *telling* them that I felt like a man swimming towards a raft in a sea full of circling fins, I constructed a cry for help masterfully disguised as a manifesto.

The story apparently had at least some of the effect desired: only a few of the listings editors and media diarists tried to accuse me of giving short change, and for a wonder nobody suggested that if I had asked the right questions Sinatra would have confessed to his long career as a Mafia button-man, handed me his gun and placed himself under arrest. But I had been too long in

Fleet Street myself to imagine that there is any such thing as a sure-fire technique for squaring the press. It will be seen in one of the *Radio Times* pieces, and in several other places in this book, how I have tried to offset the impression of being someone personally at war with the Japanese nation. No journalist who has a column to fill, however, is going to let me off the hook. The story is too easy to write.

But if the press can't be orchestrated to forgive sins, all the evidence suggests that the public can be persuaded to give the benefit of the doubt, at least until they see the actual programme. When we found out that the *Observer* piece had added a statistically significant chunk to the ratings, a bell rang. It rang louder when we realised that the listings editors – who are at their least responsible in the posh papers, strangely enough – couldn't always be relied on to give us an even break, or even a mention. (The listings editor of the *Independent* once gave an off-putting summary of a programme of ours which he couldn't have seen because we hadn't yet finished it.) Complaints would have been pointless, because to argue about the merits of your forthcoming television programme in the press is to question the authority of the public, who will deliver the only verdict that matters.

Before they can judge your show, however, they have to see it, and that's where publicity comes in. The only question is what kind of publicity it should be. The basic choice is between (a) cultivating the respect of those young media-mad invigilators who feel that they are protecting the sensibilities of a small audience or (b) getting out there where the dirt shows through the grass and whipping the big audience into the tent. I chose the latter course and now there is no way back, nor any defence except to say that whereas the consequences to a performer of identifying himself with the general public might play hob with the *gravitas*, if he believes himself separate he courts ruin.

Finally Meeting Frankie

IT WASNT the BBC's fault that the forthcoming, modest little television documentary blushingly entitled 'Clive James Finally Meets Frank Sinatra' has somehow managed to get itself hyped out of its head. The Beeb's handout merely mentioned that the show contained an exclusive interview with Frank Sinatra. That was enough for the tabloids to run breathless stories saying that the show *was* an exclusive interview with Frank Sinatra. This was very flattering and I am duly grateful, but the facts are a bit less exciting. Actually the interview lasts for about four minutes. Sinatra was in no danger of being asked a hard question and I was in no danger of being hustled roughly from the room by his overbearing bodyguards.

For one thing, he didn't *have* any bodyguards. He had arrived in Sanctuary Cove with no accompanying personnel except his musical director, his lawyers, his secretaries and a rather marvellous man who checks the details in the contract. The red carpet, for example, has to go all the way from the front door of Mr Sinatra's dressing-room to the stage, and be fixed to the floor by fasteners at no less than certain intervals. If the carpet, as it did in this case, runs along the ground instead of along the floor, it must be fastened to the ground. On the afternoon of the Sinatra concert I watched the carpet being laid and came to terms with the fact that in order to rate a red carpet fastened to the floor or ground at no less than a certain interval, it is not enough merely to appear on television. It is necessary to sing.

Sanctuary Cove is a luxury resort just north of Surfers' Paradise on the southern Queensland coast. The modest little documentary is really about Sanctuary Cove's opening week, of which the Sinatra concert was merely the – wildly successful, incidentally – culmination. The whole week was shyly entitled 'The Ultimate Event' by the man who organised it, Michael Gore. The Australian Press regularly vilifies Michael Gore as a barbarian who persuaded the ex-premier of Queensland, the notorious Joh Bjelke-Petersen, to rewrite the laws of Queensland so that Sanctuary Cove could be supplied with what amounted to a private road network paid for by the state. As subtle as a falling girder, Michael Gore's immodest personality looms large in the modest documentary. He has his weak points, but deviousness isn't one of them. Hana Mandlikova is also present, doing her best to correct my backhand. She is Sanctuary Cove's resident touring professional, meaning that she will be there when she isn't playing tennis. Arnold Palmer explains why he is still trying to get the ball in the hole. It wasn't *just* because he has been asked to design Sanctuary Cove's next golf course. It was also a matter of having been born to perform. Thus a powerful hint is given as to what compels Frank Sinatra to go on singing. All concerned in the documentary spend a lot of time assuring me, its nominal frontman, that Frank Sinatra will indeed actually turn up as promised.

On this point the tension is not entirely manufactured, because at the time it was hard to see any reason why Frank Sinatra should ever want to set foot in Australia again. He had last been there in 1974, when he had been asked many difficult questions. His response had been not to answer them. The way he phrased his refusal was, with some reason, considered rude by the Press, whose female members he called hookers. They all rushed off to look the word up in the office dictionary, after which, in the useful Australian expression, it was on for young and old. The concerts were cancelled. The unions boycotted the tour so thoroughly that Sinatra couldn't even take off to go home. He had to negotiate to get out. When he finally reached escape velocity he swore never to return.

Watching all this from 12,000 miles away in London, I thought he had a point. He was there to sing, not to be interviewed about his alleged Mafia connections, which

I suspected were rather like my Mafia connections. If I imagined myself born in Hoboken instead of Kogarah, and blessed with a beguiling voice instead of a swamp-dwelling croak, it wasn't hard to see how, if a homicidal gangster threw his arm around my shoulders and told the world I was his long lost friend, I might smile in agreement. Sinatra later made a film about Joe E. Lewis, the Chicago comedian who tried to stop working in one nightclub and start working in another. The hoodlums disapproved of the switch and indicated their displeasure by cutting his vocal cords. Sinatra played the part with fervour but it was nothing compared to the fervour with which punishment might have been handed out to him if he hadn't been fast on his feet. Yet with all that hanging over him, he had managed to give the English language its most pure voice. He sang things the way they ought to be said. In the Fifties, wearing out two copies of 'Songs for Swinging Lovers', I thought that Frank Sinatra meant democracy. He was it.

Half a lifetime later I still felt the same, and when asked to host Sinatra's return concert I didn't hesitate. I would have wanted to meet him even if he had done nothing with his life except act. Sinatra has been in some terrible movies. According to Kitty Kelly's biography of Sinatra he behaved very badly on the set of *Von Ryan's Express*, but surely the worst thing he did was to sign the contract in the first place. His carelessness about choosing film roles was always close to outright cynicism, but the reason for being annoyed with him about this was that he has always been the best naturalistic actor in Hollywood. An amateur who could rarely be persuaded to rehearse, he made the professionals look histrionic. It was the way he said things. He could pick out the rhythm of a speech so that it sounded as if he had just made it up, except that no improvisation could ever be so clear cut.

In *The Manchurian Candidate*, one of the really good films of his career, Sinatra is content to deliver the inspired lines of George Axelrod's intricate script as if they were ordinary speech. Any other actor would have tried to impose himself. By a historical irony, another of

Sinatra's films, *Suddenly*, has also been out of circulation for some time, and for the same reason – because it was about the assassination of a president. In *Suddenly*, Sinatra is even better than he was as Angelo Maggio in *From Here to Eternity*, but surely he was good enough in that to make the question of how he got the role at least marginal, if not irrelevant. There are those who are fascinated simply by the way in which Sinatra played Maggio. I myself have always been firmly in this category.

If Sinatra had never sung a note he would have been a revolutionary screen actor, but he would never have been that kind of actor if he couldn't sing. He speaks so well because of his sensitivity to rhythm – not just the rhythm of the music, but the rhythm of the words. Sinatra is, or at any rate should be, the favourite singer of anyone who writes anything, because he gets into the song through the lyric. The main reason why he sings so few recently written songs, no matter how big a hit he might have if he did, is that he doesn't think the words are good enough.

The previous fact is among those revealed in the exclusive interview, which happened just before I went on stage to host the concert. Sinatra needed to be interviewed no more than he needed a hole in the head. (Of holes in the head he probably has enough already, because according to all reports he has a hair transplant which, like the red carpet, is held down by fasteners at no more than a certain interval.) He granted a few minutes of his time because I was part of the Sanctuary Cove decor and he surmised, correctly, that I wasn't going to ask him about Joe Bananas or why he had called the female members of the Australian Press corps a dirty word.

Within these terms of reference, as the negotiators say, I found the man I expected to find. He is interested in talking about his work. He lives for it, and understands it profoundly. He is a living demonstration of the deep, awkward, unpublishable secret of all artists – that they are motivated mainly by love of what they do. Their secret is that there is no secret.

Sinatra, however undisciplined his private life has

sometimes been, is no exception to this rule. Even at the age of seventy-two, essentially he lives in order to work. Those who work in order to live – a category which necessarily includes most journalists – will always have trouble understanding that. It makes a dull story. Talking about Mafia connections is so much more exciting.

Sinatra arrived in Sanctuary Cove by private jet half an hour before the concert started and he had flown out again before the applause died. If he had stayed an extra day to enjoy the place, the Press, with the best will in the world, would have made his life impossible. The Press *had* the best will in the world because he knew them better than they knew him. He invited them to join him in a group photograph. The result was a stampede. Would-be hardbitten Australian journalists elbowed each other out of the way. Photographers took the shot and then begged journalists to take over their cameras so they could get into the picture too. It was an educational display of the sheer *force* of fame.

But the man who generates that kind of power can give it direction only to a certain extent. More often it will work against him, and all he can do is hide. At home in the US, Sinatra has his own Sanctuary Cove in Palm Springs. There he sits, walled off in his compound, unreachable by the world, with which he could stay in touch only at the minimum price of having his hand shaken until it bled.

Nobody who buys land at Sanctuary Cove will ever achieve that degree of isolation, because the security men will insist on calling him by his first name. For the brief part – about 90 per cent – of the time when this modest documentary isn't concerned with exclusively interviewing Frank Sinatra, I think it captures something of the Australian spirit. Australians are hard people to overawe, and perhaps that's why Sinatra came back – because he thought they were worth trying to impress. The $1,000,000 fee was just cab fare.

Observer Magazine
28 August, 1988

Staying Sane Aloft

LAST YEAR we sent *Postcards* from Rio de Janeiro, Paris and Chicago. This year we are sending *Postcards* from Miami, Rome and Shanghai. Six cities in two years; a flight both ways for each city; average flying time about eight hours; total flying time about four days; number of meals eaten while airborne, forty-eight. People in the air eat more often. An airline will feed you every two hours just to keep you quiet. In some of the places your aircraft passes over, people aren't eating very much at all.

Guilt-ridden and stuffed, manfully denying myself the alcohol that would bring oblivion, I have sat there wedged, all too aware that life is growing short. When I get there, filming the *Postcard* takes every hour in the day. When I get back, editing the *Postcard* is even more time-consuming than shooting it. But time in the air is time on the hands. I can read all the research again, but I have already read it pretty thoroughly before taking off. I know how many people there are in Shanghai, how many nuns there are in Rome, how many muggers there are in Miami. I could read a novel, or even write one, but at the slightest sign of either activity the stewardess will arrive with another meal.

Everything is arranged to destroy concentration. Just suppose you can master the art of reading a fat paperback one-handed while eating the steak without scattering gravy on your tie, do you think the cabin staff are going to admit defeat? They turn out the lights. It's time for the movie.

The movie is *Cannonball Run IV: The Last Gasp*. You can switch on your reading light and sit there illuminated, the lone intellectual, the only person pretentious enough to be reading *Destiny* while everyone else is watching Burt Reynolds racing his powerful wig from New

York to Los Angeles. Or you can plug in the plastic headset and succumb. So you lie there defeated, listening to a couple of actors in a sports car shouting at each other above the noise of the engine. They have that slightly demented look of performers who know they are wasting their time, and so have you. Feebly, you rebel by dialling another channel. Thus you learn that Richard Clayderman can give his personal rubber stamp even to Debussy. The aircraft is doing your thinking for you. It has you in its grip. Is there any way out?

Well yes, there is, actually, and since I discovered it, my life has taken a turn for the better. After a nightmare ride to Los Angeles, during which I went right through every audio channel twice and hated them all, it finally occurred to me that if I had my own sound system I could listen to a music programme of my own choice. I equipped myself with a top-of-the-range Walkman, featuring big padded earphones that didn't leak, so that I could play my Solti version of the Schubert Ninth at full blast without attracting a sideways glance from the man getting drunk in the next seat.

Having my own independent sound system not only transformed flying into a genuinely ethereal experience, it did wonders for my musical education. The year before last I worked my way through all the Mahler symphonies without touching the ground. The Mahler Ninth will get you all the way from London to Rome and the average Bruckner symphony is still going when you reach Singapore.

When filming a *Postcard* it's always useful to speak a few key phrases of the local language. Up in a plane with a tape plugged into your head is the ideal way to learn. The shops in the big airports have language tapes at just the elementary level you need. *Lazy Spanish* is a good one. Search the racks and you will find *French for Idiots*, *Swahili in Five Minutes* and the invaluable *Dullard's Urdu*. In Rio I was ready with the sentence in Portuguese that made all the difference when I met the muggers: 'I am with the BBC: by all means take my wristwatch, but could I have a receipt?' In Miami, where more than half the population speaks Spanish, I was able to say: 'No, I only *look* like Don Johnson.' And in Shanghai . . . ah, but Shanghai was a different story.

Radio Times
12–18 May, 1990

L.A. Lore

Los Angeles is so big, so productive, so wealthy, that if it broke away from the United States it would still have a bigger economy than India. Or do I mean Indiana? The statistics on Los Angeles are so fascinating that even I should be able to remember them, but somehow I can't. They make aeroplanes there. They make everything there. But what gets my attention is that they make stars there. Beside that glaring fact, all other facts are just data.

Millions of desperate people swim north from Mexico so that they can get jobs in Los Angeles. Some of them don't, and join gangs. The gangs go to war with each other, using automatic weapons. I should have been standing in the middle of all that with my camera crew, making an earnest documentary about the breakdown of modern urban civilisation. Why, instead, was I gripped by the idea of interviewing the barber who created Tom Cruise's hairstyle for *Rain Man*?

In Los Angeles it isn't easy to stay sane. The whole place is dedicated to making a middle-aged man with dandruff on his shoulders feel that with the right breaks and a bit of exercise before breakfast he, too, could look like Tom Berenger. Physical beauty is the norm here. All the waitresses look like actresses – and indeed, on being asked, or even before they are asked, turn out to *be* actresses, waiting for the break. Everyone is waiting for the break.

But of course they don't really *wait* for the break. They do everything they can to bring it about. Everyone is auditioning all the time. Like any other bald man in Hollywood I was constantly mistaken for a producer, since it is widely assumed that only a man so powerful would be arrogant enough to go around in daylight without a thick growth of hair, not necessarily his own, covering his skull. Consequently, every time I stopped for petrol I was assailed by some forecourt attendant loudly playing both parts in the climactic love scene from *Gone with the Wind*.

They're all at it, all the time. Supermarket checkout girls mutter speeches by Ibsen. Roller-towel maintenance engineers study horse-riding at night-school. People improve themselves until no more improvement is physically or mentally possible. *Then* they wait for the break.

Soon I, too, was waiting for the break. Instead of heading downtown to do some basic research on those gang leaders – one of them had promised not to shoot me if I gave him a signed photo of Mrs Thatcher – I found myself looking in a mirror and wondering. I wondered why, when I was so much younger than Paul Newman, that I looked so much older than Paul Newman. All right, than Paul Newman's father.

I was uncomfortably aware that in Los Angeles there is a whole service industry dedicated to helping men who feel like that do something about it. They can rebuild you from top to toe. They can even move your top and your toe further apart. All you have to do is pick up a phone.

What happened when I dialled that fatal call is the story of Thursday's film. It is the story of a man who goes in search of a dream and comes back to himself, but only after having covered the entire Los Angeles freeway system, largely on foot. See it soon at a screen near you.

Radio Times
22–28 September, 1990

News Fantasy

OUR REVIEW of the year is supposed to be a fantasy, but no fantasy could be more fantastic than the facts. This morning one of the tabloid newspapers tells me that a Taiwanese woman tourist, visiting an outlying church in the Ely area, was ravished by a curate on the floor of the sacristy. It transpires that the Taiwanese tourist, although her virtue had, in the final analysis, undoubtedly been compromised against her wishes, gave herself willingly in the first instance, the curate having led her to believe that he was personally related to the Everly Brothers. When you read something like that you realise how far even the most fertile imagination falls short of reality.

But if fantasy can't improve on the facts, it can hope to make some kind of sense of them. Our programme treats the year as a drama, with the world's leaders, celebrities, saints, frauds and cranks all featuring as characters. It's a departure from reality, but in the direction of the truth. Take, for example, that bit of film we screened last year in which Lech Walesa, after being embraced by the Pope, went away patting his pockets. We said that the Pope, an accomplished amateur conjurer, had nicked Mr Walesa's watch. A lot of people told me afterwards that they had found this to be a satisfactory gag, but couldn't quite figure out why. Agreeing with them that it was a satisfactory gag – at my age you grab whatever praise is going – I set out to explain it, to myself at least. After much wrinkle-browed analysis I came up with a partial answer. The Pope and Mr Walesa are both good men, but Mr Walesa is the more innocent. One of the reasons we admire the Pope is that he gives an air of having been around. He is a man who has lived. To acknowledge this is to strike a chord. He is in character.

Mrs Thatcher's character never showed more strikingly than on the day she resigned herself to the inevitable. In the House of Commons she slugged it out like a defeated champion who rises after the count of nine to beat up the referee. She is an historic national asset like the long bow or the tin helmet. Even her enemies are proud of her. In our version of the year, she is not only a star, she is a specific kind of star. We can call her a villainess or even a witch, but to call her a coward would not work. The audience wouldn't get it. The fantasy has to fit the character.

With President Bush this becomes a genuine problem. If you suggested that President Reagan was vague, everybody laughed, because they knew he was. Even those who admired his intelligence and endorsed his principles knew that the word 'vague' was invented for him. But President Bush, although every sentence he manages to utter scatters its component parts like pond water from a verb chasing its own tail, is not vague. The only really funny thing about President Bush is Vice President Quayle.

There again, though, the would-be fantasist must face the fact that the facts can't be beaten. We love making up things for our characters to say – the things they *should* have said – but Mr Quayle actually speaks, in real life, dialogue that no writer would dare submit to a script conference. When Mr Quayle says things like 'there are a lot of uncharted waters in space' we are hard put to keep up. Our latest review of the year is but a humble attempt.

Radio Times
22 December, 1990 – 4 January, 1991

Sidney Carton's Double Life

Sydney and London are my last two *Postcards* in a set of nine. Three years ago we started off with Rio, Chicago and Paris. Then we went on to Miami, Rome, Shanghai and Los Angeles. But in all that time the two cities I had on my mind were the one where I lived for the first twenty years of my life and the one where I've lived for the past thirty.

Sydney and London: I thought for a while of tackling the subject in book form and calling it *A Tale of Two Cities*. 'Sidney Carton, the charming but reckless son of a wealthy Sydney carton manufacturer, changes his name to . . .' But no. There was no ducking the challenge. In two programmes of just fifty minutes each, I would have to sum up my feelings about the two most important cities of my life.

It can't really be done, of course. But the advantage of the *Postcard* format is that it isn't like a letter. A *Postcard* can't, by definition, go on and on for page after page until you've got it all said. You have to pick your moments. In *Postcard from Sydney* my production team solved the problem of how to compress the whole majestic phenomenon of Sydney Harbour Bridge into a few minutes of breathtaking screen time. They made me climb to the top of it. That's where the breathtaking aspect came in; you can hear me taking every breath through a throat constricted by effort and fear.

The men who work on the bridge say that if you fall off, the impact with the water won't kill you because it's so far down that you'll starve to death before you ever get there. But it was worth the trip to the top. Sydney looks amazing from up there. I realised for the first time just how far it spreads.

When I was growing up, the first waves of post-war immigrants were arriving. Migration has gone on, and the small provincial city I knew has become a multicultural metropolis. Yet the pace of life is still far less frantic than New York or Tokyo.

On a hot Friday you can take a long lunch on the harbourside. The weekend stretches ahead, full of things to do, but always on the understanding that they should be done without raising too much of a sweat. In fact, Australia is in the grip of the biggest economic recession since the 1930s, but people have too much self-respect to blame their own work habits. Laziness is still an art form here.

London is different, although just how different had taken me half a lifetime to figure out. There are long lunches in London, too, but people are more apologetic about them. There is a general sense that the city has become a bit of a pauper. The tube trains get stuck in the tunnels because nobody can afford to grease the ratchet that holds the flange against the wedge.

Or perhaps it's just me. I arrived in Earl's Court just in time for the 1960s to start swinging. I bought a second-hand pair of winkle-pickers with toes like knitting needles, and twisted violently to Cilla Black singing 'Anyone Who Had a Heart'.

Anyone who had an eye by the time I finished dancing had to be fast on his feet. Since then, either London's pulse-rate has dropped or else mine has. If it's the latter, then the side benefit is an increased ability to linger over the stuff I really came here to get. The National Gallery, for example, is a bigger treasure house than ever when you have to walk, not run, to the nearest Rembrandt.

And what comes through, after thirty years, is the talk. Some of the best talkers in the world are in *Postcard from London*, and not all are famous. One of them is Stanley Green, the man who patrols Oxford Street with an elaborate sign warning against an excessive intake of protein.

Stanley says that eating protein causes passion, and

passion is the root of all unrest. I think Stanley has failed to realise that for some of us, the exact opposite applies: we have taken on board so much protein that passion becomes impossible.

But Stanley has a point of view, and the ideal platform to express it: London, the biggest stage in the world for all those who talk for a living.

I suppose that's why I live in London and not Sydney, but to the question 'Which city do you prefer?' I invariably reply that I'll have to think about it. Later on I send a *Postcard*.

Radio Times
25–31 May, 1991

Index